WIDNES WILD
lockdown lookback

a lookback at key moments in the history of the Widnes Wild ice hockey team as told in the pages of the *Widnes Weekly News* during the 2020 coronavirus lockdown.

ICE HOCKEY REVIEW

Published in Great Britain in November 2020 by
Ice Hockey Review
which is an imprint of
Posh Up North Publishing
Beckenham Road, Wallasey

This Edition © 2020 Paul Breeze

**All photos – unless otherwise stated –
are by official Widnes Wild club photographer
Geoff White (www.gw-images.com)**

Copyright in all materials remains with the individual authors and contributors. All reasonable attempts have been made to trace and obtain permission from copyright holders. Any infractions are completely unintentional and will be resolved at the earliest possible opportunity

All rights reserved. No part of this publication may be reproduced or copied in any manner without the prior permission in writing of the copyright holders.

British Library cataloguing in publication data.
A catalogue record for this book is available from the British Library

ISBN: 978-1-909643-40-6

Front Cover Image:
The YKK-sponsored Widnes Wild celebrate winning the Laidler Division league title in March 2019
Photo by Geoff White (www.gw-images.com)

Back Cover Images:
Wild player coach Ollie Barron celebrates the title win with fans
Wild players Lee Kemp (#15) and Simon Offord (#23) help unveil YKK as team sponsors at the start of the 2018/19 season
Wild players Ken Armstrong (#9), Tom Jackson (#84), Mike Mawer (#85) and Dan Bracegirdle celebrate milestone achievements with coach Mark Gillingham
All photos by Geoff White (www.gw-images.com)

CONTENTS

Introduction	6
Questions for the Chairman	7
Widnes Wild's First Ever Game	10
Richard Charles Looks Back At The First Widnes Game	14
Where Are They Now?	18
Craig Williams And The First Ever Widnes Wild Goal	22
Widnes Wild In The End Of Season Play Offs	24
Widnes Wild In the End of Season Play Offs – Part Two	29
Widnes Wild In The Promotion Game	38
Wild Imports – Then & Now	44
Widnes Wild In The NIHL Cup	51
Widnes Wild's Title Winning Season	57
Widnes Wild At The National Championship Game	62
Ken Armstrong – 200 Games And Counting	69
Tom Jackson's Widnes Wild Appearance Record	71
Mike Mawer Reaches 100 Game Milestone	75
Dan Bracegirdle Looks Back Over 100 Games	79
Widnes / Deeside Rivalry – Part 1	81
Widnes / Deeside Rivalry – Part 2	86
Widnes / Altrincham Rivalry	92
Widnes & Blackburn – Head To Head	98
Wild Break Records In Blackburn	104
Wild Go To Hull And Back	106
NIHL Player Award Winners	109
Bookshelf	115

INTRODUCTION by Paul Breeze

This book came about somewhat by accident and, while it is not a full and complete history *as such* of the Widnes Wild team and its players, it does cover lot of interesting aspects of that history.

Ice hockey as we know and love it ceased to operate – hopefully only temporarily – when the EIHA suspended all competitive games in the middle of March 2020 and the ice rinks were subsequently closed due to the coronavirus pandemic.

Not only did this give me - and countless thousands of other people across the country - no ice hockey to go and watch, it also gave me very little to write about when it came to doing reports for the local Widnes Weekly News.

Usually - during what people might refer to as the "close season", some of us are very busy helping at recreational games, reporting on them - and also announcing player signings for the next NIHL season. Needless to say, none of that happened this year and, with the rest of the nation's sport also put on hold, this gave the newspaper nothing to print.

We came to an agreement with the local sports editor that, instead of relying on non-existent news items, we could provide player interviews and features and look back at momentous games from the past.

Over the course of the summer, this built up quite a comprehensive bit of club history and I thought it was a shame to let it just get thrown away as fish and chip wrapping (do they still use newspaper for that..?) and decided to put it all together as a memento of the summer when nothing otherwise actually happened.

I hope you find this as interesting to read as I did to put together and that - by the time you are reading this, the crisis may have passed and there is some more ice hockey to look forward to!

  Dedicated to Michelle Thomas. And to Howard Hughes. Both veritable life savers in their own special ways xx.

Questions For The Chairman
Widnes Wild chairman Matt Lloyd explains how it all began
(Previously unpublished)

Club chairman Matt Lloyd (left of centre – holding the two trophies) - celebrating with the players and coaches after the Wild won the League and Play Off double at the end of the 2018/19 season. (Photo by Paul Breeze)

Question: What is your background in ice hockey (or sport in general…) and how did you come to be the chairman of the Widnes Wild club?

Matt: Back in 1991 I went to University and made friends with some guys who played street hockey with a team called the Leasowe Sharks.

Although I couldn't play due to my disability, I was able to get involved as a volunteer and did things like running the game clock and writing match reports and as part of our social activities we used to go and watch the Solihull Barons when the Sharks didn't have a game.

This led to a lifelong love of all things "hockey" and when I discovered the Paralympic version of ice hockey I, figuratively, jumped at the chance to play hockey.

I became the Chair of the Wild almost by default. Whilst the rink was being built it was decided that it would make more sense if the rink controlled the team and therefore, as a "local lad" it was felt I was the most appropriate person from the rink side to get involved.

Q: How did the ice rink come to be built in Widnes and at what point did the Silver Blades company become involved?

M: The council decided that they wanted an ice rink as part of the Hive and approached the owner of Silver Blades to ask for their involvement.

Q: How was the name Widnes Wild chosen and what other alternatives were considered?

M: There was a lot of discussion with names like the Wildcats and Wasps being discussed amongst other but basically Wild was my preferred choice.

Q: How were the playing colours of white and black chosen and why did this later change to yellow and black?

M: I think the original choice was made by Mick Caunce and then I decided to change the White to Yellow as it would make our fans stand out more in the crowd, especially when we were away.

Interestingly Ollie Barron designed all of the Wild kits apart from last season.

Q: How was the club logo of the black cat (panther…?) arrived at?

M: I believe this was a Mick Caunce thing.

Q: Anything else you'd like to say?

M: The key thing is that the Wild have never tried to be anyone else or copy anyone else, we have just done what we think is best for the local community.

Tom McDonald (#37) and Stewart Marriott (#14) defend the Widnes goal in the Wild's first ever game against Sheffield Spartans. (Photo by Peter Sheffield / psd-images).

Chris Preston (#47) contests a face off against Sheffield (Photo by Geoff White)

Widnes Wild's First Ever Game

First Published in the Widnes Weekly News on 11th June 2020

*Ken Armstrong in the Wild's first ever game against Sheffield Spartans.
(Photo by Geoff White)*

Sunday 11th August 2013 – Challenge Match
Widnes Wild 1 – Sheffield Spartans 6

The first ever Widnes Wild game took place on Sunday 11th August 2013 when Mark Gillingham's brand new team took on the Sheffield Spartans in a challenge match at the Silverblades Rink, as it was then known.

The choice of opposition was significant as the Spartans played in a higher division than the new Widnes team had planned to enter and would represent a considerable challenge – even more so as the game was right in the middle of the holiday period and several of the Wild players were unavailable.

The Wild team had been put together over the summer by new head coach Mark Gillingham and team manager Mick Caunce who had been in charge of the Fylde Flyers club in Cleveleys and had brought a core of players with them when that team folded at the end of the 2012/13 season. The rest of the team had been selected via a series of open player trials, which had attracted hopeful candidates from across the north west.

Aside from being the novelty of the first ever Widnes Wild game, the match was notable for several other things. Firstly, there was no spectator seating installed and the crowd had to stand round the plexi-glass – which gave for a very intense atmosphere.

Also unusual – although nobody knew it at the time – was the Wild team used the away players' bench (ie the left hand side bench when viewed from the spectators' stand). However they switched to the other bench for the next home game, two weeks later against Trafford Metros, and that has remained the home bench ever since. The only other time that Widnes have ever used the away bench was in the 2018 Laidler Division Play Off final against Sutton Sting, held at, Widnes when they were the "away" team due to Sutton's superior finishing position in the league.

A third unusual aspect to this game was that the Wild iced three netminders over the course of the 60 minutes playing time. The reason for this was that it was brand new sport being introduced to the people of Widnes and they had signed three netminders – Steve Gilmartin and Greg Ruxton who had come from Fylde and Tom McDonald, who had been signed via the player trials.

Normal ice hockey rules only allow for a team to use two netminders during a game and if both of those get injured, a skater has to come off the bench, put the pads on, and take over in goal. However, Widnes got special permission from the EIHA to be able to use all three of their netminders for this one-off game – with the agreement of the opposing team – and, as such, this is likely to be the only ice hockey match in history where this has ever happened.

Tom McDonald started off the game in goal and the rest of the team for this first ever game was:

#37 Tom McDonald (nm), #32 Steve Gilmartin (nm), #64 Greg Ruxton (nm), #4 Dan Bracegirdle, #8 Richard Charles, #10 Kurtis Hall, #14 Stewart Marriott, #19 Calum Ruddick, #21 Filip Supa, #27 Ken Armstrong, #47 Chris Preston, #58 Troy Evans, #77 Bobby

Caunce, #88 Craig Williams. Head Coach: Mark Gillingham, Asst Coach: Garry Fearon, Asst Coach: Peter Bleackley

The game started off at a tremendous pace and there was little to choose between the two teams in the opening stages.

Craig Williams scored the first ever goal for the Wild in the 11th minute – assisted by Chris Preston and Troy Evans - and the score remained 1-0 until the last minute of the period when Sheffield broke away to equalise.

With Steve Gilmartin in goal for the second period – the Spartans took the league in the 22nd minute and then edged further ahead a minute later. The Wild continued to have their own chances but with some 5 players missing from the team, they began to tire as the game went on.

In the 39th minute Sheffield scored again to make the score 1-4 at the end of the second period. Interestingly enough, that goal was scored by Nick Manning - who would later go on to play for Widnes for two seasons and be part of the Wild's play off winning team under fellow former Spartan Ollie Barron.

Greg Ruxton took over in goal for the third period but, despite plenty of passion and enthusiasm from the Wild players, higher-league Sheffield were well in control by now and two more goals for Manning rounded off his hat-trick and left the final score at 1-6 to the visitors.

Of the Widnes team that played in that first game, Dan Bracegirdle, Ken Armstrong and Tom McDonald still play for the Wild, while Richard Charles remains with the club as Assistant Coach. Mark Gillingham has also remained with the club in various coaching capacities after handing over the reigns as head coach to Scott McKenzie in summer 2015. Stewart Marriott has the unique distinction of having played in the Wild's first game but never making another appearance while the rest of the original team eventually hung up their skates or moved on to pastures new.

Looking back at the Wild's first ever game, Ken Armstrong said:

"I don't really remember much about the 1st game apart from the rink being packed and the fans were crazy. I think a lot had come straight from the Vikings game so we're fair tipsy and didn't really know much about hockey but seemed to be having fun. The 1st season went quite well for a new team. A lot of the lads already knew each other so it was good."

Dan Bracegirdle added: "I remember from the word go, the enthusiasm and commitment people around the team had. The off-ice staff and volunteers were all as committed as the players were and you could tell from the beginning there was going to be something good here for years to come. The main thing I remember from the first game was the fans! To be a brand new team and have that many people there to watch you play and making the kind of noise they made, I was flabbergasted and they haven't taken a backward step since."

And Tom McDonald chipped in:

"We played all three goalies - myself, Greg and Gilly. I seem to remember that I played pretty well and only let in 1 goal in my period. I had just returned from a training camp in Switzerland. It was a shame I didn't keep that form going into the first game of the season!"

"From my memory, we were clearly a very new team that was just learning to play together and due to that, things were a bit disorganised. The atmosphere in the rink was awesome, there were fans chanting and cheering, it was probably one of the best atmospheres I had played in, and it was a preseason game."

"I think the team put in a good show for itself against a team from the league above and we lost 6-1. Seeing how the Wild have grown over the years, I am really proud to have played in their first ever game."

Dan Bracegirdle in the Wild's first ever game against Sheffield Spartans.
(Photo by Geoff White)

Richard Charles Looks Back At The First Ever Widnes Game

First Published in the Widnes Weekly News on 18th June 2020

Richard Charles was the Wild's first ever MVP (Photo by Geoff White)

Widnes Wild assistant coach Richard Charles has been with the club on and off since the very first game – and originally joined the club as a player, having successfully negotiated the open player trials back in the summer of 2013.

It's quite an achievement to be selected for any competitive team in the first place but, if you bear in mind that Richard was actually 40 years old at the time – that makes the achievement all the more remarkable – or does it..?

A quick look at his ice hockey CV tells you all you need to know about his excellent pedigree – as he is able to boast a background that would have been pretty much unmatched in the NIHL either then or since.

Richard Charles began playing hockey at the age of 11 in Dundee as part of the Dundee Rockets junior development.

The Dundee club were the trailblazers in British ice hockey in the 1980s, winning two British League titles, three British Championship Play Off titles and one Autumn Cup and their junior system was held in very high regard.

During this period, Charles captained the Dundee U16 team to the U16 Scottish league title and the Junior British Championships at Wembley, also gaining international honours on a number of occasions for Scotland and Great Britain at U16 level.

He went on to play for the Dundee-based Tayside Tigers from 1989/90 to 1995/96 in the Scottish National League and, again during this period, gained a number of international honours with the Great Britain U19 squad, including a bronze medal at the 1991 European Championships in Sofia, Bulgaria.

He spent the 1996/97 with the Blackburn Hawks in the Northern Premier League, before returning to Scotland for the 1997/98 with the Fife Flyers in the British National League.

Unfortunately - from an ice hockey point of view – the world of work kicked in at that point and Richard was unable to commit to all the training and travelling and had to give up playing the game he loved.

So – fast forward some 15 years and Richard was now living in St Helens – just up the road from where the new Widnes rink had just opened. He attended the player trials was invited to join the team and, from there, found himself lining up for the very first game against Sheffield Spartans on 11th August 2013.

Here Richard takes up the story:

"What do I remember about the Wild's first ever game? – firstly, the crowd. I have very vivid memories of the atmosphere in the ice rink. Widnes Vikings rugby league team had played earlier that day and there were many in the crowd who had come along afterwards to see what this ice hockey was all about. "

"They had obviously been partaking in a few beers during and after the rugby and were definitely in good 'spirit' for the game. At one point there was a pyramid of beer cans stacked up against the plexi-glass and a group of bare-chested guys were singing and shouting their support, clearly enjoying themselves."

"I remember being at centre ice with one of the Sheffield lads and he turned to me and said "where have you got these fans from, this is fantastic?" From that day on it hasn't really changed."

"To hear that from someone from such an established club as Sheffield said a lot. The club has always been blessed with a lot of very supportive and committed fans and everyone at the club is truly appreciative and thankful for that. They have come on this journey with the players and officials and are most definitely a huge part of the club."

"As I got into the game, it was clear that the style had changed since I had last played. I was always a hard working, physical player throughout my career. Back then you followed through on your check, the player on the receiving end took the hit and then you then both got on with the game. You did everything you could to get hold of that puck and put it in the opponents' 'onion bag', but when the whistle went you got back to the bench or into the next face-off and started again. Not now."

"Whenever I followed through on my check I'd get a whack with a stick, or an offer to fight in return. The officials also weren't keen on this style of play and I recall getting a few penalties in the game. At this level now, not many players seem to be able to give and take a hit and the officials are very keen to penalise what I would class as fair physical play in a fast and physical sport."

"There was about 10 minutes to go in the 3rd and I went down heavily to the ice, sliding pretty hard into the boards underneath the clock. As a result of the impact I had clearly damaged my ribs and was struggling to breathe. I had to sit out a few shifts in an attempt to recover. I then had one more shift but then had to sit out the rest of the game after I got checked by a young kid and I landed on my coccyx."

"I also think that more damage had been initiated going into the boards that day. In the first league game against Deeside a few weeks later, in a very innocuous challenge, I really hurt my shoulder. The injury turned out to be a torn supraspinatus tendon. I eventually ended up on the surgeon's table and my playing career had come to an abrupt end way sooner than I, Mick, Mark and Matt had planned."

"It had been fifteen years since I had played a competitive game of hockey, back with Fife Flyers in the 1997/98 season. I was now 40 years of age. I felt at the start like I was 18 years old again, back playing the game that had given me so many pleasures and experiences over the years, with my wife Amanda and son Finlay watching me finally play the game I'd talked so much about."

"The next day I felt every day of that 40 years of age, but I had enjoyed that game so, so much, even with all the pain."

"Anyway, it turned out that I was awarded 'Man of the Match', which, of course, was a great honour for me. I assumed Craig Williams would have got it for scoring the first ever Widnes Wild goal - a great memory."

"Mick Caunce, Mark Gillingham and Matt Lloyd had pulled together a very good group of lads in a very short time to get this team off the ground and I will be forever grateful for them giving an old timer like me the opportunity to be involved back then.

"I still take great pride from my involvement with the club."

Richard Charles as player and Assistant Coach
(Both photos by Geoff White)

Where Are They Now?
by Robert Martin
First Published In the Widnes Weekly News on 18th June 2020

Kurtis Hall (left) & Troy Evans (right) (Photos by James Birtwistle)

The first ever Widnes Wild game took place on Sunday 11th August 2013 when Mark Gillingham's brand new team took on the Sheffield Spartans in a challenge match at the Silverblades Rink, as it was then known.

Of the Widnes team that played in that first game, Dan Bracegirdle, Ken Armstrong and Tom McDonald still play for the Wild, while Richard Charles remains with the club as Assistant Coach.

Mark Gillingham has also remained with the club in various coaching capacities after handing over the reins as head coach to Scott McKenzie in summer 2015, while the rest of the original team eventually hung up their skates or moved on to pastures new.

Kurtis Hall had had a long and successful career before joining the Wild in 2013/14 for what would be his final season. He played six seasons in Blackburn and joined the Lancashire Raptors for the 2008/09 season.

He spent arguably the best three seasons of his career with the Raptors; with a career high 35 points in the 2010/11 season. For the 2011/12 and 2012/13 season he played for the Fylde Flyers, before joining the Wild for their debut season in 2013/14.

Wild netminders – above: Greg Ruxton (photo by Geoff White) and below: Steve Gilmartin – below (Photo by Keith Davies)

Greg Ruxton started his net minding career at Blackburn, playing six seasons at various club levels. He joined the Lancashire Raptors for one season in 2007/08, and then switched to Fylde Flyers in the 2012/13 season.

He joined the Wild for their debut 2013/14 season and continued to play for Widnes until the end of the 2016/17 season, when a knee injury forced his retirement, posting a consistent average of .912 save percentage across four seasons.

Chris Preston made his debut for the Lancashire Raptors in the 2007/08 season going on to play three more seasons. He posted two excellent 22 point seasons during his time playing at the club, in 2008/09 and 2009/10.

He joined the Wild for their inaugural campaign in 2013/14, in which he played four consistent seasons for Widnes, including two playoff campaigns. After a successful playing career, he then went on to become the head coach of the Blackburn U15's team for the 2017/18 season.

Calum Ruddick's ice hockey career began in the 2004/05 season with the Flintshire Flames at U16 level for two campaigns. He spent some time out, before returning to play for the Flintshire Freeze in the 2010/11 season. He made his NIHL 2 debut with the Deeside Dragons for the 2012/13 season, before joining the Wild in 2013/14. He equalled a career high 12 points during the 2014/15 campaign, before hanging up his skates at the end of the 2015/16 season.

Steve Gilmartin made his NIHL debut in goal for the Fylde Flyers in the 2011/12 season, before making a trip across the Irish Sea to join the Belfast Giants of the SNL.

He made his debut for Widnes in their 2013/14 inaugural season posting a strong .854 save percentage for the season. He joined the Nottingham Lions for the 2016/17 season where he also played a great campaign.

Troy Evans began his career playing for the Blackburn Kestrels at U16 level in 2008/09, before moving up to U18 level with the Blackburn Thunderhawks. He started the 2012/13 season with the Blackburn Eagles, finishing the season at the Fylde Flyers.

He played one season for the Wild in their debut campaign, registering six points. He has played for the Bradford Bulldogs since the 2014/15 season.

Filip Supa started his career in his native Slovakia, at HC Topolcany U18's, before working his way up through the club playing at U20 level, whilst also representing the Slovakian national team.

He spent a few seasons out, before moving to England to join the Widnes Wild for their debut season. He enjoyed two excellent seasons for the Wild, posting 41 points in his debut season in the NIHL 2. He then posted a record a career high to date 80 points in the 2014/15 season. Since leaving Widnes, he has plied his trade at a variety of clubs and is now a player for the Telford Tigers.

Bobby Caunce began his career with the Blackburn Firehawks, as an U16 player, before moving up to U19 level with the Flintshire Avalanche. He made his NIHL 2 debut for the Fylde Flyers, before joining Widnes for their 2013/14 opening campaign. He then spent only two seasons away from the Wild, up until his final 2017/18 playing season, remaining a consistent performer throughout his Widnes Wild career.

Assistant coach Garry Fearon had a somewhat legendary playing career at the Blackpool Seagulls in the 1970s and 80s. He also made one appearance for the Lancashire Raptors in the 2009/10 season. After two seasons coaching with the Fylde Flyers, he became the Widnes Wild assistant coach.

Former Blackpool and Deeside netminder and Fylde junior coach netminder Peter Bleackley joined the Wild as a coach for their debut campaign and continued his role for the following season, helping Widnes in two excellent opening campaigns. After leaving the Wild, he then became the head coach of the Deeside Dragons U15's side in the 2015/16 season.

The scorer of the first ever Wild goal, Craig Williams, gave up league hockey at the of the 2013/14 season and went back to playing rec with the Widnes Wildcats. He is now a match official and was referee for the Wild's last home matches to date against Telford Tigers2 and Hull Jets in March this year - before the league season was curtailed due to the coronavirus pandemic.

Craig Williams & The First Ever Widnes Wild Goal

Above: Craig Williams (#88) scores the Wild's first ever goal back in August 2013. (Photo by Geoff White).

The first ever Widnes Wild goal was scored by Craig Williams 11 minutes into the game against Sheffield Spartans on Sunday 11th August 2013 – with Williams' name further going down in ice hockey folklore after being the first Widnes player to have a fight in a Wild game shortly afterwards.

Craig Williams actually had a background in roller hockey where he was a junior international and had also played recreational ice hockey at Altrincham, Blackburn, Bradford and Nottingham. When the Widnes rink opened at the end of 2012, he joined the Wildcats team and was fortunate enough to get picked for the new Wild league team after taking part in the player trials over the summer.

Looking back at that first ever Wild game – and his historic goal, Craig said:

"What a game to be a part of - I was just excited to be out there! Playing in front of a group of potential fans, many of which had never seen a game of ice hockey before, that was a great feeling.- could we be a small part of them getting the hockey bug?

The game is a bit of a blur apart from the national anthem, the goal and the scrap I found myself in."

"I remember thinking at the start, we are going to have to either get lucky or have a magic moment to get a goal against a well-established Division one team. It turns out that, with Chris Preston's pass, we got the bit of magic and me being in the right place, finding just the netminder to beat we got a bit of luck.

"I hit the blue line as the pass hit my stick, lucky the puck didn't fly off into the corner, but the pass was well weighted, as I put my head up the keeper moved and my shot was instinct to go low as he moved high. This was a moment that will live with me forever. A proud moment in my hockey life and one of only a few league games my Fiancée got to see me play."

Despite having made a wonder start with the new Wild team, Craig was unable to replicate that form in league games and managed just one assist in the 12 matches he played for Widnes, as he explains:

"If I am honest with myself, I did not make the grade nor fit what the coach was looking for in Widnes, and that is how it goes in sport. I went back to rec hockey and loved my time playing for Widnes Wildcats, we had a talented team with some success stories along the way in the years to come. You can see that with the number of players currently playing around the league coming from the Wildcats."

"I went on to Nottingham to play rec once the Wildcats folded and, at that point, decided it was time to find another challenge as there was no way back to league for me."

It turns out that the new challenge for Craig was to become a match official:

"I was a referee when I was younger. I covered many inline matches at senior and junior levels and loved it. I really wanted to stay on the ice and be a part of the game that I love, along with challenging myself. My goal was to reach league level. That was three seasons ago and I am now regular referee at NIHL Laidler Division level and have also had the experience of officiating in a couple of Moralee Division games."

Widnes Wild In The End Of Season Play Offs

First Published In the Widnes Weekly News on 25th June 2020

Bobby Caunce (#77) in action for the Wild in the first Laidler Division Play Off at Solihull in 2014 (Photo by Geoff White)

The Widnes Wild ice hockey team have a superb record when it comes to the end of season play off competitions. They hold the record for number of wins and are the only team in the division to have qualified in each of the 7 years that they have been held.

They have won the last three consecutive titles, but sadly missed out on the chance of adding a fourth this year when the playing season was finished early due to the coronavirus pandemic.

The Laidler Division Play Offs were introduced for the first time at the end of the 2013/14 season – the Wild's first season of competition - and were initially played at Solihull ice rink over the Easter weekend.

The idea – to mirror the Moralee Division Play off weekend which had been successfully held in Dumfries - was for the top four teams in the division to meet in two semi finals and a final to decide the overall winner.

Laidler Division Play Offs 2014 (at Solihull) 18-21st April 2014

Semi Final 1: Solihull Barons 5 – Widnes Wild 3
Semi Final 2: Coventry Blaze 1 – Nottingham Lions 2 (Overtime)
Final: Solihull Barons 3- Nottingham Lions 2 (PS)

The top four teams in the division at the end of the 2013/14 season were Solihull Barons, Deeside Dragons, Coventry Blaze and Nottingham Lions in that order but, as the play offs had not been agreed upon at the start of the season, Deeside declined to take part, saying that they had not budgeted for the extra expenditure. It was, therefore, decided to offer the final play off place to the team finishing 5th in the table, which served up a rather tasty last game of the season as Widnes had to travel to Hull to round off their league campaign and the winner of that game would secure 5th place.

The Wild won the crunch game against the Jets 4-7 and qualified for their first play off tournament. This brought with it the rather daunting prospect of facing the league champion Barons on their own ice, having lost all four league meetings between the two sides over the course of the season– with a total goal tally of 47-6.

But, previous form quite often will count for nothing in these situations and a one off game in the special atmosphere of the play offs can often bring quite a shock. It took Solihull 12 minutes to break down the stubborn Widnes defence and, while they fired in a second goal late in the first period to lead 2-0 at the first break, this was a much-improved performance by the Wild team.

Sensing the opportunity for an upset, Widnes upped their game in the second period and actually drew level with goals from Ben Brown and Bobby Caunce - and the score stood at 2-2 after 40 minutes of play.

Solihull edged back into the lead on 42 minutes but Lee Pollitt scored again for the Wild to level the score at 3-3- with just 9 minutes left on the clock. However, that was as good as it got for Widnes and two late goals from the hosts sealed the semi final win for Solihull.

The other semi-final –between Coventry Blaze and Nottingham Lions was even closer and was decided by an overtime strike having finished 1-1 after 60 minutes regulation time while the resulting final between the Barons and the Lions had to be decided on Penalty Shots.

Laidler Division Play Offs 2015 (at Solihull) - 4th 5th 6th April 2015
Semi Final 1: Solihull Barons 12 – Widnes Wild 3
Semi Final 2: Telford Tigers2 5 – Sheffield Senators 1
Final: Solihull Barons 4 – Telford Tigers2 3

The 2015 Laidler Division play offs were also staged at Solihull with the Barons looking even more impressive than they had the previous season, easily retaining their league title winning all 32 of their matches.

Telford finished second with Sheffield third and Widnes comfortably in fourth place – with 42 points from 36 games, 8 points ahead of 5th placed Deeside Dragons.

The first semi final – played on Easter Saturday - saw the Wild pitched against the Barons once again and, once again, with a "0 and 4" record to show from their league meetings during the season.

The Wild team was somewhat depleted with several players unavailable due to injury or family commitments – including key forwards Shaun Dippnall and Bobby Caunce

The game was played at a furious pace and Solihull took the lead in the 2nd minute. 10 minutes later it was 2-0 to the Barons and the score remained 2-0 at the first period break.

Danny Bullock pulled a goal back for Widnes in the 26th minute but, almost immediately, the 2-goal cushion was restored. Filip Supa pulled a goal back for the Wild but two more goals from the hosts made the score 5-2 at the second break.

Filip Supa scored again to pull the score back to 5-3 on 45 minutes but two Solihull goals within 30 seconds of each other quickly dashed any hopes of a late comeback. The Barons ran away with the game in the latter stages - having the benefit of 5 more skaters than Widnes - and scored 6 goals in the last 8 minutes to give the final scoreline of 12-3 a rather unrealistic reflection of the game as a whole.

The second semi final saw Telford overcome Sheffield Senators 5-1 to set up an intriguing "first v second" final against the Barons. This scintillating game saw a 0-0 first period and then Telford winning the second period 1-3. Solihull - who outshot Telford by 74 to 29 over the course of the game - dug deep and finally managed to pull themselves back into the game, scoring the winning goal in the dying seconds.

Wild's Pavel Vales (#26) and Lee Kemp (#15) race to keep up with Dragons' Adrian Palak in the 2016 Play Off final in Sheffield (Photo by Peter Sheffield / psd-images)

Laidler Division Play Offs 2016 (at iceSheffield) - 9th/10th April 2016
Semi Final 1: Widnes Wild 3 - Nottingham Lions 1
Semi Final 2: Deeside Dragons 9 – Blackburn Eagles 5
Final: Deeside Dragons 5 – Widnes Wild 3

The 2016 play offs saw a new venue and a new format after Solihull Barons took promotion to play in the Moralee Division for the 2015/16 season.

A decision was taken to play both the Moralee Division play offs and the Laidler Division play offs over the same weekend at iceSheffield, with 4 semi finals taking place on the Saturday and the two finals on the Sunday.

The Laidler Division season had seen a bit of an upset after Widnes had put together a very strong team headed up by new player coach and former English Premier League player Scott McKenzie with high expectations of winning the league title.

Unfortunately a set of odd circumstances saw local rivals Deeside Dragons able to ice a much stronger side than anybody might ever have imagined due to unexpected backing from the Red Hockey media group.

The Dragons won the league title finishing 8 points ahead of Widnes who, while enjoying their best ever league position to date, were still greatly disappointed with the overall outcome. Nottingham Lions finished in third place and Blackburn Eagles came fourth to take the four places at the play off weekend.

The first semi-final saw Nottingham take a narrow 1-0 lead into the first break, however, Michal Fico equalised for Widnes and the score stood at 1-1 after 2 periods.

Geoff Wigglesworth put the Wild ahead for the first time with a powerplay goal early in the 3rd period and the result was secured by an empty net goal from Scott McKenzie after the Lions had pulled their netminder in the final minute. Widnes had won their first ever play off game at the third attempt!

The other semi saw league champions Deeside see off Blackburn Eagles 9-4 to set up a 1st v 2nd final.

Deeside took a 2-goal lead but Scott McKenzie and Pavel Vales both scored to tie the game 2-2 at the first break. A poor Widnes performance in the second saw Deeside add two unanswered goals and that left the Wild too much to catch up in the final period.

The period was very close and remained goal-less until Danny Bullock pulled a goal back with 2 minutes left to play to give the Wild some hope. They pulled netminder David Good in the hope of forcing a late equaliser, however, the Dragons scored an empty net goal for a final score of 5-3 to secure the league and play off double.

Despite having had their best ever season in terms of final league position and play off performance, there was an air of disappointment around the Wild camp, having come second in both competitions to their fierce local rivals the Deeside Dragons.

Ironically, head coach Scott McKenzie upped sticks and left Widnes during the summer to take over as player coach at Deeside. He was replaced by Ollie Barron, who would go on to lead the Widnes Wild team to the most successful period in their history to date.

Widnes Wild In The End Of Season Play Offs – Pt 2

First Published In the Widnes Weekly News on 25th June 2020

Widnes Wild Captain Shaun Dippnall receives the 2017 Play Off trophy from EIHA Vice President Charles Dacres. (Photo by John Milton)

The Widnes Wild ice hockey team have a superb record when it comes to the end of season play off competitions. They hold the record for number of wins and are the only team in the division to have qualified in each of the 7 years that they have been held.

They have won the last three consecutive titles, but sadly missed out on the chance of adding a fourth this year when the playing season was finished early due to the coronavirus pandemic.

The Summer of 2016 saw a bit of turmoil at Widnes after player coach Scott McKenzie decided to de-camp and join near neighbours

Deeside Dragons, leaving the Wild approaching the next league season with no coach and an incomplete playing roster.

In came Ollie Barron who had been long term captain of the Sheffield Spartans team in the Moralee Division and who had been left without a position after his team had been unceremoniously excluded from the ice time agreement due to political in-fighting at the iceSheffield rink.

Despite having no prior experience of coaching a team, Barron was appointed player coach and arrived with several other former Spartans who were keen to carry on playing. The newcomers - with such experienced players as Stuart Brittle, Andrew Turner, Nick Manning and - later on - Simon Offord and with the outstanding young netminding talent in Matt Croyle blended very well with the existing Wild players and an exciting new team was born.

As with the previous season, there was an unexpected challenge from a hitherto unfashionable team as the Blackburn Eagles began icing imports for the first time, enticed such players as "double double" winning captain Chris Arnone away from the Moralee Division Hawks and put together a surprisingly competitive team. They won 3 out of the 4 games against Widnes and went on to win the league title by a two point margin.

Laidler Division Play Offs 2017 (at iceSheffield) - 8th/9th April 2017
Semi Final 1: Widnes Wild 2 – Altrincham Aces 0
Semi Final 2: Blackburn Eagles 1 – Sheffield Senators 3
Final: Widnes Wild 2 – Sheffield Senators 1

The 2017 Laidler Division play offs were once again played at iceSheffield as part of a bumper weekend that also featured the Moralee Division semis and final as well. The line up saw Laidler champions Blackburn Eagles take on fourth place Sheffield Senators in one semi final and Widnes pair up against local rivals Altrincham Aces in the other.

All three of the Laidler Division games were very close. The first period in the Wild's game against the Aces finished goal-less and it took until the 35th minute for Ollie Barron to edge Widnes in front.

The game opened up a bit after the goal and both sides started playing with a bit more freedom but the score remained 1-0 to Widnes at the second break.

Once they had scored, Widnes began to look the better side and were able to stamp their authority on the game. The Aces started taking more penalties and, during a powerplay for a holding call, Ollie Barron deflected a Simon Offord rocket shot past Aces netminder Declan Ryan to give the Wild a 2 goal advantage with 9 minutes left to play.

The remaining minutes were very scrappy with both sides picking up penalties and the Wild had to do without the services of Berwyn Hughes and Stuart Brittle who both picked up 2+10 minute penalties for checking.

The Wild's game had followed the form book as they beat third place finishers Altrincham Aces 2-0 in the early morning game but the second semi-final was a different story.

The Eagles had finished a massive 10 points ahead of fourth place Senators in the final Laidler table and had a 2-1-1 record against the Senators. They would normally have been expected to be firm favourites to reach the final but the Eagles' preparations for the play offs had been overshadowed by a dispute with their home rink over ice time arrangements and sponsorship for the new season and this may have taken its toll on the players.

As it was, the Sheffield Senators – playing on their home ice – raced into a 0-3 lead by the first break and the game was effectively over after just 20 minutes. Although the Eagles outshot the Senators by 41 to 31, their finishing was certainly below par and Mark Hartley played a blinder in the Sheffield goal.

A goal for the Eagles just after the mid-point of the game did little to change their fortunes and ended up being little more than a consolation.

In the final on the Sunday, the Wild were quickest out of the blocks and put Sheffield under pressure right from the first drop of the puck. The Senators looked sluggish and had probably used up a lot of energy reserves in their game the day before and it was no great surprise when Widnes took the lead through team captain Shaun Dippnall after 11 minutes.

What was more of a surprise was that the score remained 1-0 at the first break and it was not until 23.12 on the clock that the Wild scored again – with player coach Ollie Barron picking up a rebound and firing the puck into the Sheffield net to double the Widnes advantage.

Widnes were by far the better team at this point – looking likely to score again at any moment – and it was only due to the shot-stopping heroics of Mark Hartley in the Sheffield goal that the score was kept down.

Sheffield finally managed to drag themselves back into the game with a goal by Elliott Knell after 45 minutes and the rest of the match was played on a knife-edge. The Senators looked much better going forward by now and Widnes had to work hard to protect their single goal lead.

The clock ticked down without further incident and Widnes were able to celebrate the perfect end to their best ever season so far in which they had achieved their best ever league position, finishing just 2 points behind league champions Blackburn Eagles, and brought Ollie Barron a piece of silverware in his first season as a player coach.

Above: Goal action from the 2017 Play Off Final against Sheffield Senators (Photo by John Milton)

Widnes Wild celebrate winning their second play off trophy in a row after the first tournament to be held in Widnes in 2018 (Photo by Geoff White)

Laidler Division Play Offs 2018 (at Widnes) - 14th/15th April 2018
Semi Final 1: Sutton Sting 4 – Telford Tigers 3
Semi Final 2: Widnes Wild 6 – Hull Jets 5 (PS)
Final: Sutton Sting 3 - Widnes Wild 6

The 2017/18 season saw the Barron-led team ready for another challenge for the Laidler Division title and this time around they were undone by the decision of Sutton Sting to drop down from the Moralee Division for the season. As it happened, Widnes actually won three of the four league meetings between the two sides but were eventually undone by poor results against lower table teams and ended up in second place in the table once again, 7 points behind champions Sutton.

The other two play off places went to Hull Jets – who finished in third place, level on points with the Wild - and Telford Tigers who finished one point behind.

There was a new format for the play offs this season with the Moralee competition having quarter finals, semis and final played as home and away ties but the Laidler teams opted to keep with the single weekend arrangement.

The Planet Ice rink at Widnes was selected as the venue with the two semi finals being played on the Saturday and the final on the Sunday.

The Wild had to come from behind in their semi-final game against the Hull Jets, trailing 2-5 at the mid-way point of the game before fighting back to draw 5-5 at the end of the third period and forcing the game into overtime.

The extra 5 minutes of play produced no "golden goal" winner so the tie went to a penalty shoot-out – the first one ever seen at Planet Ice Widnes. The score was tied at two penalties each after three attempts and it actually took 4 more rounds of "sudden death" shots – due to the inspired shot-stopping skills of both Wild's Matt Croyle and Hull's Dean Bowater – before the two teams could be separated, with the Wild's Shaun Dippnall firing in the winning penalty much to the delight and relief of team-mates and fans alike.

The other semi-final saw Sutton Sting beat Telford Tigers 4-3 to set up a champions v runners up battle for the coveted play off title.

In the final on the Sunday, the Wild got off to a good start – after a very tense opening phase – with goals from Danny Bullock and Nick Manning to take a 0-2 lead into the first break. However, they were pegged back with two quick strikes by Sutton early in the second period – on 22 and 25 minutes – but a well-taken second goal of the game for Manning re-established the Widnes lead some 90 seconds later.

There was no more scoring in the second period but Sutton looked increasingly threatening and, had they not incurred penalties at crucial moments, might have made more of their chances.

A 4th goal for Widnes just 90 seconds into the third period, courtesy of Andrew Turner, gave the Wild a bit of breathing space - but the Sutton attack continued and they scored on 52 minutes to narrow the gap once again to a single goal and set up a fascinating last few minutes.

The Wild defended furiously in this closing phase and managed to keep the Sutton offence at bay. A goal by Stuart Brittle with just 3 minutes left to play pretty much settled the game and the win was made certain, after the Sting had pulled their netminder in favour of an extra attacking player, with an "empty net goal" by hat-trick man Nick Manning in the dying seconds.

The Wild celebrate their third play off crown after the 2019 final at Widnes
(Photo by Peter Sheffield / psd-images)

Laidler Division Play Offs 2019 (at Widnes) – 20th /21st April 2019
Semi Final 1 (4.30pm): YKK Widnes Wild 9 – Bradford Bulldogs 3
Semi Final 2 (7.30pm): Telford Tigers2 1 – Hull Jets 4
Final: Widnes Wild 6 – Hull Jets 3

The 2018/19 season was case of "third time lucky" for Ollie Barron and his men as they finally secured the Laidler Division title that had previously eluded them.

The Wild finished top of the league 6 points ahead of runners-up Telford Tigers, with the other play off places going to third place Hull Jets and Bradford Bulldogs - who had qualified for the first ever time.

The Laidler Division Play Off weekend was staged at the Planet Ice rink in Widnes for the second year running – with two semi finals on Saturday and the final on Easter Sunday.

The first semi final saw Widnes beat Bradford Bulldogs in a high-octane encounter which, despite being very close for much of the game, eventually finished 9-3.

Bradford actually scored first in the game and, while Widnes fought back, the game remained on a knife-edge with the score finely balanced at 3-3 at the half way stage.

Two goals late in the second period finally gave the Wild a bit of breathing space and then 4 unanswered goals in the third ensured the win for Widnes, albeit with a scoreline that was probably a little harsh on the battling Bradford side.

The second semi final saw league runners up Telford Tigers2 take on third place finishers Hull Jets in an incredibly tense game between two very closely matched teams. Hull scored the only goal in the first period and then made it 0-2 by the end of the second. The Tigers pulled a goal back early in the third period and looked as if they might stage a late rally but they got caught out at the back while pushing forward and Hull scored twice more in the closing stages to win the game 1-4.

In the final on Sunday between Widnes and Hull, Wild player coach Ollie Barron helped settle any early nerves by firing the Wild into the lead after just 5 minutes of play. A second goal followed from Danny Bullock with just 60 seconds left in the period and the Wild took a 2-0 lead into the first break.

Widnes scored three more goals – from Tom Jackson, Jakub Hajek and Ross Jordan – to build up a healthy 5-0 lead before Hull finally managed to find the back of the net in the 37th minute.

The Humbersiders noticeably upped their game after this breakthrough and two more strikes for the Jets in the third period set up a nerve-jangling finale.

The last 5 minutes were all Hull as they laid siege to the Widnes goal, with netminder Matt Croyle and the dogged Wild defence performing wonders to keep the puck out of the net.

The Jets removed their netminder for the last 60 seconds of the game to allow for an extra attacking player and, but with just 20 seconds left on the clock, the Wild's Jakub Hajek broke out of defence and skated the length of the ice to fire in an empty net goal, which finally put the result beyond all doubt.

The Wild's third play off win in a row, added to the Laidler Division championship title, represented an impressive haul of trophies from player coach Ollie Barron's three seasons in charge at the club – even more so as he had no coaching experience before taking over the reins at Widnes in the summer of 2016.

Following this success, Barron decided to step down from his position as player coach and retire from the game on high note.

He was replaced by Mike Clancy who began a rebuilding process to put together a new look Widnes team based around youth and development.

Unfortunately, the season was one to forget and the Wild only finished fourth in the Laidler Division table, although they did qualify for the Play Offs for the seventh season in a row, they did not get the chance to defend their title as the event had to be cancelled due to the coronavirus pandemic.

Above left: Wild player coach Ollie Barron receives the MVP award in what was his last ever game for Widnes and (right) team captain Simon Offord receives the Play Off trophy from EIHA Vice President Charles Dacres (Photos by Paul Breeze).

Below: Wild trophy celebrations. (Photo by Peter Sheffield)

Widnes Wild In The Promotion Game

First Published In the Widnes Weekly News on 13th August 2020

Whitley Warriors built up a commanding lead in the home leg of the 2015 Promotion Play Off game (Photo by Geoff White)

The Widnes Wild Ice Hockey team has enjoyed considerable success in recent seasons, having won three play off titles and also the League title - but one area in which they have yet to make any sort of inroads is the promotion play off game, in which they have taken part on three occasions and have yet to be victorious.

The Wild's first involvement in the promotion game – or, to give it its correct title The Promotion/Relegation Play Off – came at the end of the 2014/2015 season when they had finished a very creditable fourth in the Laidler Division table.

At the time, the League rules called for a team that had finished second in the Laidler Division to play off against the team that finished second bottom in the higher Moralee Division, home and away over two legs, with the winner playing in the higher division the following season.

Because of a re-structuring of the League that season, three teams – Solihull Barons, Telford Tigers and Sheffield Senators all gained automatic promotion from the Laidler Division so Widnes, with their fourth place finish, were invited to take part in the promotion game.

It has long been widely acknowledged that there is a significant gap in team strength and playing standards between the two NIHL North Divisions, so the likelihood of a Widnes side who had only finished in fourth place in the Laidler Division having much of a chance against a Moralee Division side – even one who had only managed to finish second bottom of the League – was rather remote.

The tie saw the Wild paired up against the Whitley Warriors, who have a long and distinguished history going back to the 1950s and who have always produced a superb batch of home-grown players.

Promotion / Relegation Play Off 2015 (Two Legs)

11th April 2015 (at Planet Ice Widnes)
Widnes Wild 3 – Whitley Warriors 9

12th April 2015 (at Whitley Bay)
Whitley Warriors 11 – Widnes Wild 2

In the home leg – played at Widnes on the Saturday - the game began at a furious pace but early goals from a skilled and physical Whitley Warriors, put the home side on the back foot.

Despite a number of great stops from Great Britain Ladies netminder, Nicole Jackson, the power and accuracy of the visitors' shots, took the game away from Widnes and it was Whitley's ability to quickly change defence into attack, which was the home side's undoing. A disappointingly small crowd, including a noisy visiting contingent, were shocked by a 0-4 first interval lead.

Two goals inside the opening three minutes of the second period appeared to prompt a netminding change for Wild, with Greg Ruxton taking his place between the pipes.

Wild opened their scoring on 23 minutes, with the influential Bobby Caunce finding the net, assisted by Filip Supa and Shaun Dippnall.

However Ruxton couldn't prevent a remarkable goal from Adam Reynolds at 24.07. From there on in, a rejuvenated Wild took the game to their renowned opponents.

In the 26th minute Shaun Dippnall added a second for the Wild on the powerplay. End to end play brought the crowd to their feet but it was the visitors who added an eighth goal in the 39th minute - Greg Ruxton making a brilliant reaction save but the resulting rebound being fired high into the net by Martin Crammond.

The final period saw two tiring sides, matching one another in goals with Ben Richards scoring from close in for the Warriors and Bez Hughes adding a final goal for the Wild. The dominance of the visitors was emphasised in the period shots on goal totals - 26 to 11 in favour of the Warriors.

Sunday's return leg saw a determined Widnes team open well. Greg Ruxton was selected in goal and, despite confusion in the Wild defence leading to a Dean Holland opener for Whitley in the 2nd minute, the visitors grew in confidence. Daniel Bullock was put clear by Sam Dunford in the eighth minute and he rounded netminder Mark Turnbull to equalise.

A big and noisy Wild visiting support nearly lifted the roof. Their noisy encouragement was in evidence throughout. Within three minutes Wild took a sensational lead when some fine interpassing from Dippnall and Caunce led to Filip Supa finding the net. Widnes held the lead until the last seconds of the first period when a low shot beat a screened Greg Ruxton.

Netminder Ruxton produced real heroics in the second period, foiling dozens of Warriors raids but he was beaten by several shots coming through a crowd of players. With the end of second period score at 6-2, Wild battled hard on tiring legs to shut down a home team keen to add to their goals total. After taking an incredible 64 shots, Greg Ruxton gave way to Nicole Jackson to see out the last ten minutes.

Although heavily outshot, Widnes battled through to the end with Bez Hughes and George Crawshaw close to scoring in the last three minutes.

Wild v Sheffield Spartans in the 2016 Promotion game at Blackburn

Photo courtesy of Colin Ellis (from video footage)

Promotion / Relegation Play Off 2016 (Single Game)
16th April 2016: at Blackburn Arena
Sheffield Spartans 5 – Widnes Wild 0

Following their second place finish in the Laidler Division table behind champions Deeside Dragons at the end of the 2015/2016 season, the Wild once again qualified for a promotion play off place. This time the opponents were the Sheffield Senators but, on this occasion, due to a lack of ice time available at iceSheffield for the away game, it was agreed to play the match as a one-off tie at a neutral venue – in this case, Blackburn Arena.

This was the first time that a promotion playoff had ever been played as one-off game in this country and it attracted attention from across the ice hockey world, with live coverage on NIHL Radio and lots of fans of other teams going to Blackburn to watch the game.

As things turned out, fortune favoured the Moralee Conference side as the Spartans took the lead as early as the 3rd minute and never really looked like losing after that. They outshot the Laidler Conference runners up by 40 to 24 and picked up what was their first win since the middle of January.

Widnes – despite having prepared well for the tie with recent NIHL North Cup games against Moralee opposition in the shape of Blackburn Hawks, Solway Sharks and Billingham Stars – were unable to make any impression on a stubborn Spartans defence and endured their only competitive shut-out of the season.

Bez Hughes (#20) celebrates his equaliser in the 2017 promotion game against Deeside (Photo by Geoff White)

Promotion / Relegation Play Off 2017 (Single Game)
2nd April 2017 (at Blackburn Arena)
Deeside Dragons 4 – Widnes Wild 3 (after Overtime)

The Wild's last foray into the promotion game brought with it their closest result to date. The team were buzzing following their first ever trophy win in the Laidler Division Play Offs and, with the promotion game pitting them against local rivals Deeside Dragons, there was much to play for. Once again, the match was played as a single winner-takes-all tie at Blackburn Arena.

It was the third time in 3 seasons that Widnes had qualified for the promotion game, having lost 5-0 to Sheffield Spartans in a one-off game played at Blackburn last season and 20-5 on aggregate over two legs to Whitley Warriors back in 2015.

As might be expected for a game of such importance, the opening phase saw some robust plays by both teams and a number of penalties were handed out before the Dragons took the lead through Jordan Bannon in the 6th minute.

Towards the end of the 1st period, Wild's Danny Bullock had to leave the game injured after a clash with Dragons' Simon Furnival who was given a match penalty.

This handed the Wild a 5 minute powerplay and then Deeside picked up a 2 minute penalty for too many men on the ice which gave Widnes a 5 on 3 advantage – and they made the most it with Bobby Caunce scoring a fine goal on 18.42 to level the score.

Despite starting the second period with a man advantage, Widnes were unable to make any further headway on their powerplays and a goal by former Widnes player Filip Supa put Deeside back into the lead 2-1 on 23.12.

The lead did not last long however and Wild equalised again on exactly 29 minutes after Nick Manning carried the puck into the Dragons' zone and, with no passing options, just dumped it towards the goal and it sneaked inside the post past netminder Denis Bell.

The Dragons continued to pick up minor penalties and Widnes put huge pressure on the Dragons goal on the powerplay – but then, on 36 minutes, the Dragons raced down the other end and Jordan Bannon fired past Matt Croyle in the Wild net to make it 3-2. The Wild players' heads did not go down, however, and on 38.45, Wild player coach Ollie Barron fired in a fierce shot which rebounded off Bell and Bez Hughes fired in to equalise for the third time.

With the scores tied at 3-3 after 60 minutes of play, the game went into a 5-minute period of sudden death overtime where the first team to score a goal would win the game. Overtime is played with just 3 skaters on the ice from each team instead of the usual 5, with no imports allowed.

The Dragons put the Wild goal under extreme pressure and it took several great saves by Croyle to keep Widnes in the game. They seemed to have weathered the storm and a fierce shot from Andrew Turner rattled the Dragons' goal post but then – with just 1.50 left until the game would go to a penalty shoot-out, Wild's Stuart Brittle picked up a 2 minute slashing penalty.

This meant that Widnes would be a man short for the rest of the game and the pressure finally told with just 51 seconds left on the clock as the Dragons scored the winning goal that would keep them in the Moralee Conference for another season.

Wild Imports - Then & Now

First Published In the Widnes Weekly News on 16th July 2020

Wild imports Jakub Hajek and Michal Novak celebrate the title win with Mike Mawer (centre) (Photo by Geoff White)

The Widnes Wild team finished last season with 3 overseas players on their roster after German forward Daniel Haid was signed in January as an extra imported player.

Haid was signed partially as cover while Michal Novak was getting over a long term injury and also to take some of the pressure off Jakub Hajek and allow Widnes the option to rotate their players in the run up to what was expected to be a thrilling title battle.

Unfortunately, things did not work out as planned as the league season was cancelled with several crunch games left to play - but not before Daniel had made an impact on the Laidler Division, scoring 7 goals and 6 assists in his first 11 league games.

Haid hails from Bietigheim in Germany and spent 4 season playing for the Chemnitz Crashers in the minor German leagues, scoring

24+37 in 55 league games. He has more recently been studying at Sheffield Hallam University where he played for the Sheffield Bears student team.

The 2019/20 season was certainly an odd one for the Wild team. It began with high hopes of the retain the league title that they had won the year before and also bagging their 4th play off title in a row - but all manner of things went wrong.

The team struggled for much of the season with key players out with long term injuries and playing lines often had to be cobbled together depending on who was available for each game. This saw leading scorer Hajek playing with different players from week to week and it was very creditable that he still managed to notch up 20 goals and 30 assists for the season.

Novak had a good pre-season, scoring 7 goals in 4 challenge matches but then missed much of the league campaign after picking up an injury. He managed to battle back to fitness and played 6 league games before the competition was curtailed, scoring 4+2.

Following on from the superb previous title winning season that had seen both Hajek and Novak in flying form, scoring 41+39 and 26+30 respectively, it was all a bit of a disappointment but such is the nature of ice hockey - you never know what is going to happen next!

Wild's Daniel Haid (#44) lines up to score against Deeside Dragons from an incredible kneeling position. (Photo by Hannah Walker)

Widnes have been lucky with their choices of import in previous seasons - and not so in others... Here's a run down of previous overseas players to have iced for the Wild, starting at the very beginning.

Filip Supa (#21) away at Deeside (Photo by Geoff White)

Filip Supa (Seasons 2013/14 – 14/15)
Widnes Wild Record: 37 games, 22 goals, 42 assists, 72 Penalties In Minutes (PIM)

Filip Supa was the Wild's first ever import signing, joining the team for the debut 2013/14 season. Having learned his hockey at the Topolcan club in his native Slovakia, playing over 100 competitive games at Under 18 and U20 Level, he then spent several years away from the game.

When the new Widnes rink opened, Supa was living in Warrington. He came along to the open player trials and was offered a place on the Wild team for their first season. He went to be top goal scorer for the season with 27 strikes in 22 games and returned for the following season, where he scored an incredible 55+25 in 34 leagues games.

Having been a huge favourite, with the Wild fans, Supa blotted his copybook somewhat by moving to join arch rivals Deeside Dragons for the 215/16 season.

He played in North Wales for two seasons and has most recently been icing for the Telford Tigers 2 team where he remains one of the top goalscorers.

Widnes Assistant Coach Richard Charles played with Supa in the Wild's first ever season. He said of the Slovakian:

"He was a good hard working player with a real determination to dig deep offensively. He was a very quiet player but effective. A good goal scorer, he maybe just didn't get the service he would have liked in that first season but he and Bobby Caunce eventually clicked very well and formed a powerful partnership. Given that he was the first import the club had, there was a lot of pressure on his shoulders and he relished the limelight and was a real fans favourite. He aspired to bigger things and ultimately that's why he left."

Wild import defenceman Pavel Vales (#26). (Photos by Geoff White)

Pavel Vales (Seasons 2014/15 to 17/18)
Widnes Wild Record: 113 games, 20 goals, 61 assists, 68 PIM

Born in Brno in the Czech Republic, Pavel Vales was already living in Widnes when he came to the attention of the Wild club.

He had learned his junior hockey with the Karlovy Vary juniors teams and played some 240 competitive games at Under 16 and Under 18 level before graduating to play for Teknika Brno and Boskovice in the minor Czech leagues.

Aged just 22 when he joined the Wild, Vales played for Widnes for 4 seasons as an import defenceman, making 113 competitive appearances in the Laidler Division, Play Offs NIHL Cup.

He was a very solid and reliable player was widely considered as one of the best skating players in the league. He was part of the team that won the Laidler play off title in 2017 and again in 2018 and was named in the divisional All Star Team for the 2016/17 season. In the 2017/18 season, Vales scored the most assists by a defenceman (25) in the division.

He sustained a serious facial injury in game away to Blackburn in the 2015/16 season and had to wear a strengthened full face mask after that to protect his face. While he continued to put in superb performances for the Wild for two more seasons afterwards, this obviously had a deep effect on him and he retired from playing the end of the 2017/18 season.

Talking of Vales, Richard Charles said:

"Excellent hands, excellent skater, excellent player - he brought lots to the team both offensively and defensively and he could skate backwards faster than many could skate forward. His gap control as a defence man was exceptional and he wore his heart on his sleeve and did everything for the team to win. Again, very quiet, but he had a strong, controlled aggressive side to him. He was a fantastic passer and shooter of the puck, again very controlled."

"Pavel reminded me of an old import, Jaroslav Lycka, who played for Dundee Rockets and then Lee Valley Lions. The incident at Blackburn really affected him. It was the most horrendous incident I have experienced in all my hockey career and he felt really let down in terms of support from the powers that be outside the club."

"Had that not happened I personally think he would have played longer with us, possibly still with us. Although very quiet he was a great character within the team and when he did speak/comment he was very funny. He was also a joy to coach and to have him as part of coaching staff, particularly around the juniors would be a real asset to the club."

< Photo by Geoff White

Michal Fico
(Seasons 2015/16 – 16/17)
Widnes Wild Record: 37 games, 22 goals, 42 assists, 72 PIM

Following the departure of fan favourite Filip Supa to local rivals Deeside Dragons in the summer of 2015, new Wild player coach Scott McKenzie offered the vacated import berth to Michal Fico.

The Slovakian born forward was already known in Widnes as he had been playing for the Widnes Wildcats recreational team for the past two years.

Despite the obvious step up in playing standard and the fact that he had no prior league experience of any note in his home country, Fico had a good debut season in NIHL hockey, scoring 20 goals and 18 assists in 33 league and cup games and he re-signed for the following season under Ollie Barron.

Unfortunately, Fico suddenly upped and left Widnes after just one league game of the new season and joined Laidler Division rivals Blackburn Eagles. The Eagles went on to have a very good season – surprising many by winning the league title – although Fico's contribution as their second import was only 5+24 in 22 league games.

Fico was last seen playing for the Deeside Dragons 2 team in the 2017/18 season where he was their top scorer with 20+16 in 24 games, although he got into serious penalty trouble at the end of the season and has not played competitive hockey since.

Richard Charles said of Fico: *"He had ability but didn't really stand out over the home grown players in the team, as an import should, in my opinion. He was hard working, but would get very frustrated at times if things weren't quite going his way. He had a number of run-ins with team-mates in training, but that didn't worry me, as it just showed his determination to win the puck. "He was always in the shadow of Supa which, I think, affected him. Because of all that he wasn't really a team player, more of an individual."*

Elvis Veldze (Season 2017/18)
Wild Record: 8 games, 11 goals, 2 assists, 4 PIM

At the time of his signing in the summer of 2017, Elvis Veldze was the only import to arrive at Widnes with any sort of NIHL playing record behind him, having previously played a season for the Fylde Flyers, scoring 35+21 in 30 league games.

The arrival of the 6'5" former Latvia Under 21 international player caused quite a lot of excitement around the club but it was to be short lived.

After scoring an impressive hat trick in his first game - an 8-3 preseason win over Bristol Pitbulls – Veldze found his work commitments made it difficult for him to get to training and games and he only managed to make 7 appearances in the league, adding 8+2 to his scoring tally.

Elvis Veldze (#42) in action for the Wild against Coventry Blaze.
(Photo by Geoff White)

Widnes Wild In The NIHL Cup
First Published In the Widnes Weekly News on 23rd July 2020

Above: Wild's Jakub Hajek celebrates a goal in the home cup defeat to the Solihull Barons in the 2019/20 NIHL Midland Cup competition. (Photo by Geoff White)

The Widnes Wild ice hockey team entered the NIHL North cup competition this season for the first time in 5 years - and it was quite a bold step as the team was in a rebuilding phase following the retirement of former player coach Ollie Barron and a lot of player turnover during the summer months.

Incoming head coach Mike Clancy heralded the move and as one of the first steps in his three year plan to build a team that would be capable of regularly competing at a higher level and it was to be quite a test as the competition involved the Laidler Division Wild team taking on 4 teams from the higher Moralee Division – Blackburn Hawks, Solihull Barons, Sutton Sting and Nottingham Lions – on a home and away basis in the qualifying group.

With the widely acknowledged step up in playing standards between the two divisions, this was always only ever going to be a "toe in the water" exercise to assess relative team strengths but it did turn out to be a fascinating voyage of discovery.

In fact, the Wild did better than they had ever expected – holding the Blackburn Hawks to a 5-5 draw at the end of regulation playing time before narrowly losing out in sudden death over time – and then taking Nottingham Lions to a penalty shoot out decider, after having drawn 5-5 in normal time in the Lace City. This was the first time that the Wild had ever taken points off higher league opposition in a competitive fixture and as such, was cause for celebration.

Close games at home to the Lions (2-3) and Sutton Sting (1-3) also brought lots of positives and the Wild were only really outclassed in their two matches against the Solihull Barons, losing 3-9 at home and 13-2 away.

As a bit of background information, it is worth pointing out that unlike in, say, football where "the cup" has a particularly set of traditions and part of the fun is seeing who progresses to the next round and who they might be drawn against, running any sort of cup competition in ice hockey tends to be more difficult.

This comes from the fact that ice time for all the fixture dates have to be agreed at the start of the season – and to fit in with all the other teams that use the rink as well as the overall league fixture schedule – and this makes it difficult to accommodate a pure "knock out" cup competition. In fact, the last time the British ice hockey actually attempted to run a knock out cup – back in the 1990/91 season, it petered out after the first round of matches as nobody could work out how to play the latter rounds.

Therefore, in order to reduce fixture confusion the only manageable way to hold a cup competition is to have a qualifying group or groups with just the winners going to compete in the final stages

Despite having its own - relatively - long standing Challenge Cup, even British ice hockey's Elite League doesn't have a proper cup competition as such as they count the first league meetings between all respective teams towards the cup and arrive at the initial qualifying group from those results.

Thus, with many teams at NIHL level either having problems getting extra ice time at rinks or, indeed, operating as a purely "development only" team with little support to finance extra games, cup competitions tend to be organised on a season by season basis depending on which teams what to enter.

The only previous occasion that the Wild had entered the cup competition was in the 2015/216 season when Scott McKenzie was head coach and the opposition were reigning Moralee Division champions Blackburn Hawks, Solway Sharks and Billingham Stars.

In a possibly slightly over-optimistic interview looking ahead to the cup games, McKenzie said;

"This will be a fantastic competition for the Wild to be a part of. Whilst we will be the underdogs it's our intent to win the NIHL North Cup. It's never been a secret that the Wild are looking to win promotion to the Moralee Conference at the end of the season and playing in the Cup will give the guys a taste of playing at that level in competitive games".

"Pre-season we played the Solihull Barons and the Blackburn Hawks so we know the standard that is expected and we also showed we were able to compete with teams at that level."

9th January 2016: Billingham Stars 7 - Widnes Wild 3

The Wild's first cup game – and first ever visit to Billingham - saw an incredibly entertaining match with 7 goals being scored in the first period. Billingham took the lead after 3 minutes but Scott McKenzie equalised for the Wild 4 minutes later afterwards. Michal Fico cancelled out a second Stars strike before Billingham edged 4-2 ahead. Chris Preston pulled the Wild back into contention with a great goal on 18 minutes but that was the best of the action as far as Widnes were concerned.

A 5th goal for Billingham straight after the restart edged them further ahead and further goals either side of the second period break handed them a 7-3 victory.

27th February 2016 Blackburn Hawks 12 - Widnes Wild 2

The visit to the home of the current Moralee Division league leaders and reigning champions always looked to be a somewhat daunting prospect, especially with Widnes having already lost there 9-0 in a pre-season challenge game.

As it turned out, the Wild defended doggedly and it took until the 12th minute for Blackburn to open the scoring. They went 2-0 up on 15 minutes but the Scott McKenzie pulled a goal back for Widnes making the most of a mix up in the Hawks defence. The hosts scored again for 3-1 at the end of the first period but there was still hope for the Wild.

Any hopes of remaining in the game were dashed as Blackburn scored just 51 seconds from the restart and raced to an 8-1 lead by the mid-point of the game. Wild's Shaun Dippnall scored an excellent breakaway goal to pull the score back to 8-2 but 4 more unanswered goals in the third period rounded off an easy win for the Hawks.

6th March 2016: Widnes Wild 1 - Blackburn Hawks 7

The return game against the Hawks ran pretty much to script with the Wild battling well but having trouble making any sort of headway against the league leaders.

The visitors opened the scoring on 7 minutes and 5 more goals in the ensuing 10 minutes –including two within 25 seconds of each other and a Penalty Shot – saw the game pretty much over as a contest by the first period break.

In a much closer second period –which the Wild actually "won" 1-0 - Danny Bullock scored the only Widnes goal of the game on 28 minutes. This was followed by a spate of fighting that saw three Blackburn players – including former Widnes captain Ben Simister - handed 10 minute major penalties, along with the Wild's Tom Jackson and Chris Preston.

The only goal in the third period came for Blackburn on 50 minutes to give them a 1-7 lead and, while a defeat is still a defeat, the Wild were able to take solace from the fact that this had been their closest result to date against the Hawks first team.

27th March 2016: Widnes Wild 2 - Solway Sharks 8

The visit of Solway Sharks saw the first ever England v Scotland encounter at the Silver Blades rink and Widnes put in a very good performance against the former Moralee Division champions. The score was a ver narrow 0-1 to Solway at the end of the first period but early two goals for the visitors in the second edged them further ahead.

Above: Three Toms in action for the Wild – Thomas Ratcliffe (#40), Tom Jackson (#84) and Tom McDonald (nm #37) against Billingham in the 2015/16 NIHL North Cup. (Photo by Geoff White)

A great goal from Michal Fico on 31 minutes finally got the Wild on the score-sheet but two more goals followed for Solway and saw them leading 1-6 at the second period break/

Two further goals came for the Sharks in the third period before Thomas Ratcliffe fired in the second Wild goal of the night after 50 minutes to round off the scoring for the evening.

2nd April 2016: Solway Sharks 5 - Widnes Wild 1

The Wild's first and - to date - only ever trip to Scotland saw them travel to Dumfries to take on the Solway Sharks and, with no league netminder available for the trip, Widnes Wildcats recreational keeper Ian "Budgie" Thirkettle was called into action for the game.

The match started at a frantic pace with the Wild looking very good against the Moralee Conference 4th placed Sharks. They actually took the lead with a well-worked solo goal by George Crawshaw and the score remained 0-1 to Widnes at the first period break.

Two quick goals early in the second period put Solway in the lead and although the Wild outshot the hosts in that middle third, the score remained 2-1 at the second break. Ian Thirkettle put in a superb display in goal, facing 44 shots overall and only seeing 5 go past him and the Sharks finished off the scoring with a 2-0 third period for a final score of 5-1.

3rd April 2016: Widnes Wild 1 - Billingham Stars 7

The Wild's last game in the 2015/16 NIHL North Cup competition was always going to be a bit special as, with the way the fixtures had turned out, the Billingham Stars would move to the top of the group and win the cup if they won the final game at Widnes.

A defeat, however, for the Stars would mean that Blackburn Hawks would remain top of the group and would win the cup instead, having already completed all their group games. While it always looked likely that the Stars would pull this off, there was still a job to be done and the game attracted quite a lot of interest from across the ice hockey world – and had live match commentary broadcast by NIHL Radio.

Despite the eventual scoreline, this was a very closely balanced game for a lot of the time. Tom McDonald performed heroics in the Wild net to keep the Stars attack at bay and it took until the 16th minute for them to score their first goal. Although Billingham then scored again just two minutes later for a 2-0 scoreline at the end of the first period, Widnes could be pleased with their efforts. Two more goals followed for the Stars in the second period and then, with two more early in the third, it looked as if they already had one hand on the cup.

Widnes finally managed a consolation goal with a great effort from Thomas Ratcliffe in the 55th minute and Billingham rounded off the scoring with a late strike with just 90 seconds left on the clock.

A delighted Billingham team – backed up with a sizeable travelling support – were presented with the NIHL North Cup – their first trophy since the won the league title in 2012 - and Widnes were able to look back on an interesting first foray into the cup competition.

Widnes Wild's Title Winning Season

First Published in the Widnes Weekly News on 6th August 2020

*The Wild players, staff and fans celebrate the club's first league title win
(Photo by Geoff White)*

The YKK sponsored Widnes Wild's league title ambitions were finally realised in the 2018/19 season after having been thwarted so many times before. Having finished as runners up in the Laidler Division for the three previous seasons, everything finally fell into place at the right time for player coach Ollie Barron and his team.

The announcement of a new main sponsor for the season in the shape of world renowned manufacturing company YKK provided a huge boost to the club and the good news just went on from there.

Most of the previous year's squad were back for another go at the title – apart from popular import defenceman Pavel Vales and Sheffield-based forward Nick Manning, who had both given up playing.

The squad was boosted by some exciting new faces. The most notable was Czech import Jakub Hajek, who had played the previous season for Altrincham Aces. He had scored 26+19 in 30 games for the Aces team that had finished 5th in the league table and promised much.

The Wild opted for the first time to go with a second import forward in Michal Novak. Novak had never played in this country before and had not played competitively anywhere since 2012 so was pretty much an unknown quantity in NIHL terms. However, he had come with a very good pedigree having learnt his junior hockey in his native Czech Republic – a Pool A World Championship nation - and played some 230 junior games and over 200 senior games in the Czech minor leagues.

Another newcomer to the Wild team was 18 year old Daniel Fay, a graduate of the excellent Bracknell junior system with experience of playing for the Bracknell Bees and Hornets teams in NIHL South. Fay was starting at university in Liverpool and had been offered the chance to join the Wild after impressing in summer training sessions.

The Wild defence was further strengthened with the arrival of two players with a lot of higher league experience. Scott Cooper joined from Solway Sharks, with over 100 games behind him at Moralee Division level, having also had spells with Billingham and Whitley and with Slough Jets in NIHL South.

Ross Jordan also moved south across the border, having spent the previous seasons playing for the Edinburgh Capitals and Paisley Pirates in the Scottish National League. Prior to that he had been an old teammate of Ollie Barron for a number seasons, having played for the Sheffield Spartans in the Moralee Division.

The season actually started in a rather low-key fashion with a 2-9 home defeat to Sutton Sting in a challenge game. That's not quite as bad as it sounds, however, as the Sting had been gearing up for higher league hockey and it was their fourth game of their pre-season programme while, for Widnes, it was the first run out with all these new players on board.

The league season began with an exciting close 4-3 home win over regular bogey side Sheffield Senators and then a 3-7 victory in the return game at iceSheffield a week later.

Another narrow home win over early season league leaders Bradford Bulldogs saw Widnes move up to second place in the league table and things were beginning to look promising.

The wheels came off the hoped for title challenge with a 2-0 defeat away to Telford Tigers and then a 4-2 defeat away to Hull the week after. The ship was steadied with a record equalling 22-2 win over the Blackburn Hawks development team at Planet Ice Widnes and then the Wild finally moved to the top of the league table with a narrow 3-5 win away at Bradford that saw them leapfrog the Bulldogs.

These back to back victories helped kick-start a 100% run that would see the Wild win 17 games in a row – a club record – and set them well on the way to securing their first ever league title.

This run included a morale boosting 2-1 win over main title threat Telford Tigers, an incredibly narrow 0-1 win away in Hull and then back to back wins over Bradford to well and truly scupper their own title ambitions.

By the turn of the year, the Wild had built up a commanding lead at the top of the Laidler Division, 9 points ahead of, by then, second place Sheffield Senators.

Jakub Hajek was flying in the goal scoring stakes and was the Division's top goal scorer with 25 goals from 19 games. However, the Wild were far from being a one-man team and player coach Ollie Barron had weighed in with 19 goals from 19 games and Mikey Gilbert and Michal Novak (both 14 goals) and Danny Bullock (9 goals) had also made a huge contribution to the offensive unit.

In terms of playmaking, Barron had the highest number of "assists" in the season to that point with 25, Gilbert and Hajek have 20 each and team captain Simon Offord – a great steadying influence in defence – had 15.

The winning run continued until the end of January when the Wild were caught out once again at Telford – losing 4-3 – to keep the Tigers in with a slim chance of still being able to catch up on points.

Three more victories put the Wild back on track, only for the pre-championship party to be spoiled once again by Telford who won 2-5 in Widnes in mid February – the first home defeat since the friendly game against Sutton back in August and the only other home defeat overall in the season.

Further wins followed over Hull and Altrincham and, while it had looked fairly clear cut for much of the latter part of the season, the Wild picked up the points that would finally make them un-catchable in the league standings with a 4-1 home win over the Aces on 17th March.

Local pride was guaranteed with a 5-9 win away to Deeside and then a 16-5 home win over the same opposition in the last league game of the season. That meant that the Wild had managed a clean sweep of 4 victories in all 4 league games over both the Dragons and the Aces for the first time ever.

The Laidler Division trophy was presented to team captain Simon Offord in a special ceremony after the game and fans were able to join the players on the ice afterwards to take photos and get involved in the celebrations.

The Wild finished top of the Laidler Division table with 56 points from 32 games. That represented 27 wins, 1 overtime win and 4 defeats. The four defeats came at the hands of Hull Jets (once) and Telford Tigers (three times), meaning that the Tigers actually held sway over the Wild in terms of meetings between the teams, if not in league table placings.

The Tigers ended up in second place in the table, 6 points behind Widnes, with 5 defeats and 4 overtime losses (1 point awarded for drawing at the end of the regular 60 minutes playing time) to their record. Hull were a distant third with 45 points and Bradford fourth with 41.

Player coach Ollie Barron was the Wild's top points scorer for the season with 33 goals and 44 assists from the 32 games. He actually finished third overall in the Laidler Division scoring standings behind Sheffield Senators' Thomas Humphries - who finished with 36+52 - and Telford's Callum Bowley with 30+49.

Jakub Hajek was the overall top goal scorer in the division with 38 strikes – level with Deeside's James Parsons – and 35 assists, significantly improving on his previous season with Altrincham where he had only managed 45 points albeit playing with an arguably weaker team. Michal Novak had a good first season in British ice hockey with 26+30 while Mikey Gilbert had his best season to date in terms of points with 52 overall, beating his previous year's tally by one.

Wild first choice netminder Matt Croyle was the division's top netminder for the second season in a row - ending the campaign with a 92.02% save percentage. Across the 28 league games that he played in, he conceded just 55 goals from 689 shots - ahead of Bradford Bulldogs Phil Pearson who finished in second place with 91.57% (878 shots / 74 goals).

Winning the NIHL North Division2 title meant that Widnes were pitched up against the South Division 2 champions Slough Jets in a one off game to decided an overall national Division 2 champion. The game was played at Coventry on 14th April as part of the "Final Four" weekend that also included the national play offs for the Division1 North and South teams as well. Unfortunately, it turned out to be a bit of a day to forget for the Wild fans who travelled down to the Midlands as Widnes lost 1-7 to an impressive Slough team.

Luckily the fans had something to cheer about the following weekend as the Laidler Play Offs were staged at Planet Ice Widnes for the second year in a row. Widnes beat Bradford Bulldogs 9-3 in the first semi final and then saw off Hull Jets 6-3 in the final to their third Play Off crown in a row and notch up an historic league and play off double triumph.

The Wild secured the league title with their 4th league win of the season over the Altrincham Aces (Photo by Geoff White)

Widnes Wild At The National Championship Game

First Published in the Widnes Weekly News on 13th August 2020

Wild's Chris Gee (#46) scored the only Widnes goal against Slough in the championship game at Coventry (Photo by Geoff White)

Following their historic Laidler Division title win at the end of the 2018/19 season, the YKK-sponsored Widnes Wild qualified to take part in the NIHL Division 2 National Championship game. This was a relatively new fixture in the ice hockey calendar and, to date, has only ever been played twice - so being only one of 4 teams ever to have taken part in the national N2 final, the Wild are part of a very select club.

Since the launch of the modern British League in 1982, club ice hockey in Britain at its highest level has always been played on a national basis. The current Elite League has regional conferences but an overall national league structure and the new, second tier, NIHL National Division is, by its own definition, also a "national" division.

From 1982 onwards, the British Championship (a completely different trophy and title to the "British League league champions" title) has been decided by a play off weekend held at a big venue at the end of the regular season. It started off at Streatham ice rink in 1982 with Dundee Rockets seeing off Blackpool Seagulls, Murrayfield Racers and the home Redskins team to become the first modern day winners and, over the years, many traditions have grown up surrounding the event.

The lower levels of British ice hockey have always been operated at a regional level to cut down on travelling distances and costs for teams with limited budgets and resources and, therefore, the league competitions have been split between NIHL North and NIHL South.

Both the NIHL North and South Division One competitions (known as the "Moralee" and "Britton" Divisions and both named in honour of previous ice hockey administrators) have always had their own play off competitions, with the top finishing teams in the league playing home and away legs to arrive at an overall winner - but these have always been kept separate between the north and south.

There was, for a while, a meeting between the two champions of the North and South Division 1 leagues but this died out over time as teams variously claimed they couldn't get the ice time at their rink on such short notice (in all fairness, who knows back in August that they are going to win the title at the end of the following March…) or they didn't have enough players available because they all had holidays booked, or their imports had already flown home - or whatever.

However, after the demise of the English Premier League (national tier 2 competition) in the summer of 2017 after several teams had left for various reasons leaving the competition with too few teams to remain viable, the leftover sides joined either the Moralee (north) or Britton (south) Divisions - depending on their location - and, because the EPL had always had a national play off weekend in the past, the appetite was there to come up with a new type of event to finish off the season.

It was decided that both the expanded North and South Division ones would have their own separate league championships and then home & away play off competitions but that, following all of that, the top two teams in each would meet in Coventry in April for a "Final Four" weekend to decide an overall national play off champion. The two semi-finals were to be played on the Saturday and the final on the Sunday and, in order to pad out the programme somewhat and to include more teams and attract more fans to this new gala event, it was decided to invite the winners of the two regional Division 2 leagues – the Laidler Division in the north and Wilkinson in the South - to take part in a new Division 2 National Championship game – the first time this had ever been done.

The first such Division 2 game took place at the inaugural "Final Four" weekend in Coventry in April 2018. This saw North champions Sutton Sting take on South champions Oxford City Stars with the result being a very close 1-3 victory for the Wilkinson Division winners.

The Wild had visited the Coventry Skydome Arena on many occasions before, playing against the Coventry NIHL Blaze in the Laidler Division, and had not lost there since their debut 2013/14 season - but this was a special one off game at a neutral venue being played in front of a sizeable crowd of fans from mixed teams and so was very much an unknown quantity.

Prior to the Coventry game, Widnes had never played a competitive game against a team from NIHL South before – although they had played two pre-season challenge games in the past against the Bristol Pitbulls, winning once and losing once.

In fact, they did not even know who they were going to be playing against in the National Final until the last of the NIHL South Division 2 Wilkinson league games, which were only completed the weekend before.

The South 2 title race was incredibly close and finished with both Slough Jets and Solent Devils locked on 51 points at the top of the final league table but, as Slough had won both games against the Devils – 3-1 at home and 8-3 away on successive nights back in October – it was the Jets who were able to claim top spot based on results between the two teams.

The top points scorers for the Jets in the Wilkinson Division were Lukas Smital with 27+57 in 19 games and Sean Norris with 35+44 in 24 games and they finished in 4th and 5th place in the overall scoring standings respectively. Before moving to Slough in 2017, Czech born Lukas Smital played over 500 games in the North American minor professional leagues and 550 games in the EPL for Guildford Flames and Bracknell Bees and added a huge amount of experience to an otherwise relatively young team.

Before the game, Wild's Daniel Fay – who had previously spent his whole playing career at Bracknell before joining Widnes the summer before - when asked about the differences between NIHL North and South said:

"There are a few differences between the North and the South – mainly being the physical aspect of the game. Back home (ie NIHL South…), the hitting aspect of the game isn't really focused on much so, even though I took the occasional hit, I have definitely been hit much more this season."

Widnes netminder Mall Croyle was to come up against some familiar faces as he had learned his junior hockey with the Slough club before moving to Sheffield and had played with and against a number of the current Jets team. Upon arrival at the Coventry arena, he discovered that he actually had his own mini fan club among the Slough fans who remembered him from his time at the Berkshire club and had put together flags and banners bearing his name!

As to the match itself, while it was a obviously a privilege for the North 2 champions to be involved in this one-off game against the South 2 champions, it will probably be looked back on as a bit of a disappointment overall. Slough had the upper hand for long periods of the game and, when Widnes did have their chances, they weren't able to make them count.

That said, the first period was, in fact, very close and Widnes had the chance to take the lead after Jakub Hajek was felled while bearing down on goal and he was awarded a penalty shot. Unfortunately, his attempt was blocked by the Slough netminder's pad and the first goal eventually went to the Jets in the 17th minute.

Slough edged further ahead early in the second period and were 4-0 up before Chris Gee finally put the Wild on the score-sheet with just under 2 minutes to go to the second break.

Any hopes of a third period rally by the Wild were dashed by another Slough goal just two minutes from the restart – the fifth from the same player, Sean Norris – and insult was added to injury with two more goals within 20 seconds of each with five minutes left on the clock, which rounded off the scoring for the game at 1-7 to the Jets.

Despite the eventual result, Wild player Chris Gee still has fond memories of the game:

"I remember the atmosphere was good. It was loud with the bigger crowd but still not the same atmosphere as being at Widnes - even though we have fewer people at the games."

"Before the game everyone looked calm and composed in the changing room and we were all having a laugh. We had a decent warm up and felt excited to play and I feel like the score didn't tell the real story of the game. We did play well, but not to the best of our ability, even though we all still worked hard and wanted to be there - but sometimes these things happen."

"I personally think if we got to replay the game, it would have ended as a different result, as we were definitely a good enough squad to get the job done, even though on that particular day it didn't fall that way."

Looking back at his goal – the only goal that Widnes scored in the game, Gee said:

"During the game, I personally felt fit, strong and confident. In my mind, my job was to put the pressure on the other team as much as I could and be the workhorse chasing down everything in sight."

"I remember the goal. We had been putting pressure on them in their zone and, as the puck was shot in I remember skating towards the net. As I looked at their goalie, I noticed he had left a gap on one side. As the shot missed the net, the puck bounced off the back boards and I knew that all I had to do was to get a touch in as quickly as I could whilst there was still a gap."

"So, without over-complicating anything, I just went for it and, once I saw the puck go in the net, it was an awesome feeling to get a point on the board for the lads to keep some wind in our sails!"

Looking back at the D2 National Championship game, Wild Assistant coach Richard Charles said:

"These are the kind of games as players you should relish and rise to. Unfortunately I think the significance of the event took over the team a bit. The biggest thing I can remember - and which I personally thought deflated the team - was the news that Michal Novak had come down with a stomach bug overnight and wasn't going to be able to play. He was clearly a big part of our strike force and we did look to him and Jakub, as our imports, to really rise to such games and, when they do, you then hope that the rest of team follows. Jakub worked very hard - maybe too hard at times - and got a little frustrated, which is understandable."

"There was nothing to be intimidated about in this game I felt. There was no pressure on us as a team. We were clearly the underdogs, but more than capable to cause an upset. Over the years I have thought that as a team, we just don't believe in ourselves enough and this was another example."

"We didn't really single out anyone in their roster. Obviously Smital brought a wealth of experience to Slough and he was clearly their leader, old head and calming influence both on and off the ice. With the slow start that we had, a door opened for Norris and he capitalised with a fantastic performance scoring 5 of their 7 goals."

"In games like this, you need to do something significant early doors, be it a goal, a good play, a hit, but something to get the other team on the back foot and thinking 'hold on'. We just didn't have that. Chris Gee's goal was obviously significant and lifted morale, but again it just came a little late."

"We just didn't make an impact early enough and we played catch up the whole game. I recall myself, Ollie and Mark having a final rally of the troops in the second interval and the boys gave everything in that third period but it was just too late. The score in my opinion did not reflect our performance, our fight or our capability, but the belief just wasn't there. That comes with experience and Smital's presence certainly brought that out in the Slough team."

"It was a great experience and the feeling of losing shouldn't be forgotten, but be brought to mind in future games to drive the belief and success of the club forward. A mentality of 'Winning isn't everything, it's the only thing' has to be the mantra. It did put a little damper on the success we had over the season, but two golds and a silver is something that I was, and we should all be, very proud of."

The advent of the new NIHL National Division (2nd tier) for the 2019/20 season saw another reshuffle in the end of season play off arrangements across the divisions.

It was decided that the "Final Four" weekend would continue at Coventry as before with the top teams from two qualifying groups meeting in semi finals and final. The Moralee, Britton, Laidler and Wilkinson north and south divisions were to have their own play off weekends – held at Sheffield, Bracknell, Widnes and Alexandra Palace respectively - with the top four teams from each league meeting in straight semis and final. The plan was for the winners of the North 1 play off weekend at Sheffield and the South 1 event at

Bracknell to meet up in a new one-off Division 1 National Championship game at the Coventry weekend, as had been done with the D2 teams in the two previous years, although there was no mention of continuing with the Division 2 version this time around.

As things turned out, in the wake of the coronavirus pandemic, it was all rather academic as the ice hockey season was curtailed in mid-March and none of the proposed post-season play off events took place.

MATCH DETAILS:
Sunday 14th April 2019 – National D2 Championship (at Coventry)
Widnes Wild 1 – Slough Jets 7
Period Scores: 0-1, 1-3, 0-3
Shots on Goal: Widnes 33 – Slough 45 (11-12, 12-20, 10-13)
Penalties In Minutes: Widnes 20 – Slough 16
Widnes Scoring: Chris Gee 1+0, Bez Hughes 0+1

MVPs: Widnes – Danny Bullock / Slough – Sean Norris

Full Widnes Wild Line-Up: Luke Wilson (NM), Daniel Bracegirdle, Oliver Barron, Ken Armstrong, Daniel Bullock, Scott Cooper, Lee Kemp (AC), Michael Gilbert, Daniel Fay, Bez Hughes, Simon Offord (C), Stuart Brittle (AC), Barry Sprakes, Matthew Croyle (NM), Chris Gee, Jakub Hajek, Ross Jordan, Tom Jackson, Mike Mawer, Shaun Dippnall

View From The Bench – a shot showing the Wild players warming up and the Wild fans cheering them on at Coventry. (Photo by Richard Charles)

Ken Armstrong
200 Games and Counting!
First Published in the Widnes Weekly News on 7th May 2020

Wild's Ken Armstrong (#9) celebrates the title win with wife Amanda. (Photo by Geoff White)

The recent 2019/20 season saw four Widnes Wild players reach important milestones in their playing careers, with Ken Armstrong and Tom Jackson reaching 200 appearances for the Wild and Dan Bracegirdle and Mike Mawer both notching up 100 games.

"King" Ken Armstrong is a highly popular personality around the club and has been there since the very first game back in August 2013. Having originally played his junior hockey at Altrincham, he played some 80 English League games for the Lancashire Raptors and Blackburn Eagles teams before joining the brand new Widnes set up 7 summers ago.

Back then the Raptors and the Eagles were "development teams" – rather like the current Blackburn Hawks2 team - and were geared up to giving younger players experience of playing rather than challenging for trophies and, as such, they tended to struggle at the bottom of the league year in year out.

Commenting on his decision to join the Wild, Armstrong said:

"After playing at Blackburn for a few years and not winning many games I had the chance to come to Widnes and play with one of my best mates who I'd never had the opportunity to play hockey with (Calum Ruddick). So we both signed for Widnes - and then Blackburn went on to win the league…!"

Looking back to that first game - which ended up as 1-6 defeat to a highly experienced Sheffield Spartans team – he said:

"I don't really remember much about the first game, apart from the rink being packed and the fans were crazy. I think a lot had come straight from the Widnes Vikings Rugby League game so were fairly tipsy. They didn't really know much about ice hockey but seemed to be having fun. The first season overall went quite well for a new team. A lot of the lads already knew each other so it was good."

Armstrong has seen many players come and go over the seven seasons that he has been at the Wild - but who were the best…?

"That's a hard question because we've had a lot of really good players over the years that have all had different impacts on the team in different ways. The best individual player would be Scott McKenzie. But then when Ollie Barron, Stuart Brittle and Nick Manning were playing together they were very impressive."

Asked about his favourite memories from his 200+ games at Widnes, Ken said:

"My favourite memories in my time with the Wild would be winning the league title and playoffs and also the team nights out we've had because it's a really good group of lads."

By the end of the current 2019/20 Laidler Division season, Ken Armstrong had notched up an incredible 220 games for Widnes Wild, scoring 21 goals, 28 assists and picking up 48 penalty minutes.

Talking about his award for having passed 200 games, he said:

"Getting to the 200 games milestone is something I'm proud of and couldn't have done it without all the coaches that picked me for the team. Hopefully I can carry on playing and add to that."

Tom Jackson's Widnes Wild Appearances Record

Wild defenceman Tom Jackson (#84) (Photo by Geoff White)

Popular Widnes defenceman Tom "TJ" Jackson's long service at the club was rewarded recently with a special award to recognise 200 appearances as a Wild player.

Jackson actually has the highest number of appearances overall for the Wild team with 225 under his belt – despite not having been at the club as long as some of the other players - and that is quite an achievement for a player who is only 24 years of age!

Jackson learnt his junior hockey in Hull and played over 70 games at U16 and U18 levels for Kingston junior teams, as well as making 4 appearances for the North U15 Conference representative side.

He played his "rookie" NIHL season in 2012/13 with the Hull ENL Stingrays (as the nowadays Hull Jets team were then called) making

15 senior appearances while still turning out for the Kingston Under 18 team as well.

The 2013/14 season saw the big switch as far as Tom was concerned as he started off the season on Humberside playing 15 games for Hull before opting to join the new Widnes Wild team mid-term. He played 15 games for the Wild – scoring 2 goals and 2 assists, picking up 46 penalty minutes – and has been here ever since!

Tom explains how that move came about:

"My time at Hull was great, coming through the last few years of juniors and starting out at seniors I got to play with some great players and got really good coaching from their system. When I came to Widnes there were a number of factors which brought me to the team."

"First of all was the realisation that ice hockey is not a cheap sport, I'm lucky enough to have been supported even through a majority of my senior years by sneaky gifts off my mum and dad after breaking sticks and other parts of kit. Travelling to Hull from my home town was rather expensive 4-5 times a week when it became senior hockey."

"Secondly, I had just started working at a temporary ice rink in Manchester city centre so I was able to fund my travelling expenses to Hull for hockey, also working at that same ice rink were a couple of original Wild team members who I became rather close to such as Calum Ruddick and Tom Ratcliffe and they helped in the decision to switch sides and come to Widnes."

"I also knew Shaun Dippnall from growing up and playing roller hockey and this gave me more of a reason to be able to join a team mid-season knowing a few people already - especially at a younger age."

"Lastly and most importantly was the team itself. Everyone involved with the Wild was so welcoming and, even before I had left Hull, being able to train with the Widnes team before I made the decision. I was also able to come to a few games and seeing how the fans would get behind the team blew me away."

When asked about which players had impressed him to most in his 6½ seasons at Widnes so far, Tom said:

"It's hard to just pick one person, there has been many players and coaches that played their part over the years. The first few years, the coaching staff were great to start us along the path to winning ways coached by Mark Gillingham, who kept that consistency throughout. Scott McKenzie brought in great coaching systems and made us into a more professional outfit and then Ollie Barron turned us into that winning team who won the 3 playoff titles and then the league title last season."

Commenting on the past season, Jackson said:

"This season was always going to be tough, if you remove a whole top line from any team in any league it leaves a big gap to fill by other players. Starting the season was exciting with new faces and coaching and then we started getting injuries but showed our character in games to battle and get out of each game with points, even with a depleted team."

"Once we got back a few more players toward the end of the year, we were having a nice little run before it all got put on hold and cancelled in a tough way, leaving us a bit bitter how the seeding happened with points being dished out for games not being played previously and then not for the last few games but it just gives us more to play for next year."

"Personally I just do what I can to help the team if the teams winning and I feel I'm contributing that's all that matters for me."

Tom's younger sister Charlotte took up ice hockey this season after a number of years playing roller hockey and ball hockey and immediately won the league title with the Widnes Wild women's team in her debut season. How does he feel about that?

"The women's team have really improved this season and proof is in their achievement of winning the league. It's great that she's now playing and enjoying it, she tried when she was younger and couldn't stand up and she's only really started on ice this season too - so she's really doing well."

"She's stubborn but I often go on and help the women's training and it's good to keep an eye on her and make sure, if she's not concentrating, I can give her a shout or even a little whack across the pads to wake her up again!"

By the end of the current 2019/20 Laidler Division season, after 6 ½ seasons with the Wild, Tom Jackson had notched up an incredible 225 games, scoring 16 goals and 47 assists.

The 6'2", 214lb defenceman is no shrinking violet and has 307 penalty minutes to his name – a total which is "bettered" (if you choose to look at it that way..) only by Lee Kemp who has 365 PIM from 175 games and Thomas Ratcliffe with 326 PIM from just 114 games.

In terms of total appearances for Widnes, Jackson leads the way with 225, followed by Ken Armstrong on 220 games, Shaun Dippnall on 197 games and then Bez Hughes and Lee Kemp – both with 175 games.

Talking about his award for having passed 200 games, Jackson said:

"It feels like I'm ageing, but it's great to play in front of our fans and being around the boys in the changing room. I'm just grateful that I've been able to keep coming back to the team to play for the coaches, players and the fans."

Tom Jackson with sister, Wild women's player, Charlotte and Mother - and match night volunteer - Nicky. (Photo by Geoff White)

Mike Mawer Reaches 100 Game Milestone

First Published in the Widnes Weekly News on 21st May 2020

Wild's Mike Mawer (#85)– fondly known as "Biff". (Photo by Geoff White)

Popular Widnes forward Mike Mawer was one of the group of players who crossed the Pennines in the summer of 2016 to join player coach Ollie Barron's new look Wild team, after their Sheffield Spartans team had been unceremoniously pushed out of existence at its iceSheffield home.

Mawer was born in Grimsby and learnt his junior hockey there on the infamously compact playing surface, playing for the Redwings Under 16 and Under 18 teams.

He joined the Sheffield Senators for the 2012/13 season in Division 2 North and remained with them for three seasons, playing 83 games and scoring 19 goals and 4 assists.

For the following 2015/16 season, he stepped up a division and played for the Sheffield Spartans team in Division 1 North, playing 34 games and scoring 3 goals.

By a strange twist of irony, the last Spartans game that Mawer – or, indeed, any of the Spartans players – played in was promotion play off game against Widnes on 16th April 2016, staged at Blackburn Arena. The result was a disappointing 5-0 for the Wild and saw the last appearance of player/coach Scott McKenzie in a Widnes shirt.

The Sheffield team that day contained 5 players – Ollie Barron, Will Barron, Andrew Turner, Stuart Brittle plus Mawer – who would very shortly become Widnes players, although nobody knew that at the time.

As history has now recorded, Ollie Barron's 3 season tenure at Widnes was the most successful in the club's history so far – winning three play off titles and one league title - and Mawer was, obviously, a significant part of that team.

As an ice hockey player with the nickname "Biff", Mike obviously has a physical side to his game – as his penalty minutes tally per season of 36, 62, 42 and 44 can confirm

Away from the Wild, Mike was selected to represent the British Universities team at the World Student University Winter Games in Almaty, Kazakhstan in early 2017. Mike was also conditioning coach for the Team GB Women's Under 18 teams at the World Championships in Katowice, Poland in January 2020.

By the end of the current 2019/20 Laidler Division season, after 4 seasons with the Wild, Mike Mawer had played 126 games, scoring 20 goals and 29 assists, with 184 penalty minutes.

PB TRANSLATING

Over 30 years' experience of translation & interpreting in industry & commerce - specialising in English / French /German.
Also involvement with Italian, Spanish, Dutch, Russian, Czech & Polish.

For enquiries, please e-mail to pbtranslating@gmail.com

Dan Bracegirdle Looks Back Over 100 Games

First Published in the Widnes Weekly News on 14th May 2020

Wild's Dan Bracegirdle (#4) with father Dave and mother Kathy
(Photo by Geoff White)

Widnes defenceman Dan Bracegirdle was one of the original core of players to form the team back in the summer of 2013 and he was rewarded recently with a special award to recognise 100 appearances as a Wild player.

Bracegirdle had been playing with the Fylde Flyers ENL team in Cleveleys along with player coach Mark Gillingham and when that team suddenly folded at the end of the 2012/13 season and Gillingham was offered the job of head coach at the new Widnes rink, it was natural that he would he bring a number of the Flyers players with him to build a team around.

Along with Bracegirdle came Bobby Caunce, Andrew Clark, Troy Evans, Anthony Melbourne, Dan Etherington, Joe Charlton, Kurtis

Hall and netminders Greg Ruxton and Steve Gilmartin and, of that original contingent, Dan is the only one still playing for the Wild.

Blackpool born Bracegirdle learnt his junior hockey in Blackburn but didn't actually play any competitive senior hockey until the Fylde Flyers first season 2011/12. He played 47 games for the seaside team over 2 seasons, scoring 4 goals and 2 assists from his defensive role before joining the Wild.

He missed the 2015/6 and 16/17 seasons through illness but bounced back to become an important part of Ollie Barron's play off and league title winning side.

Dan played in the Wild's first ever game – a challenge match against Sheffield Spartans on 11th August 2013 – and went on to have successful first season with the fledgling Wild team. Looking back to that first season, he said:

"I remember from the word go the enthusiasm and commitment people around the team had. The off-ice staff and volunteers were all as committed as the players were and you could tell from the beginning there was going to be something good here for years to come."

"The main thing I remember from the first game was the fans! To be a brand new team and have that many people there to watch you play and making the kind of noise they made, I was flabbergasted and they haven't taken a backward step since."

"The season as a whole was a successful one I'd say for our first. We made the playoffs in Solihull and established a good enough reputation to build year on year over the following seasons."

Talking about his favourite memories with the Wild, Bracegirdle said:

"There's a few for sure! I think it's hard to top winning the league and the playoffs in the same year, that was really special. Winning the playoffs the season before that meant a lot though too as that was the first trophy I was part of with the club and the presentation nights after both of those have been pretty memorable."

"On an individual note, I don't pop up with too many goals so the one away from home against Nottingham less than 4 seconds into the game I won't forget, as well as the game winner against Deeside at home in the 14/15 season."

"It's no secret around the rink that I'm not Deeside's biggest fan so to score the winner in a derby game at home meant a lot as I'm sure most people could tell from the celebration."

When asked about which players had impressed him to most in his time at Widnes so far, Dan said:

"There have been lads that have played a few seasons here that I've played on the same teams as a lot throughout my life so the performances that those players like: Bobby Caunce, Shaun Dippnall and Greg Ruxton put in never really surprised me over the years."

"In terms of guys I'd never played with before, there's a long list of players I could reel off especially from the past few seasons when we've won both the league and playoffs - players I'd even played against in the past and didn't realise how good they actually were. Watching lines like Brittle, Barron and Manning a few seasons back or Bullock, Novak and Dippnall last year, the way those guys clicked was really impressive."

"That being said there's guys, like TJ (Tom Jackson) and Bez (Hughes) who have been here from early on and who have developed over time into really good players that could play high up on any team in the league now - or even try their hand in the league above - and to see the commitment to improving from those guys has been really impressive too."

Reflecting on the Wild's season this year, considering all the various upheavals, Bracegirdle said:

"You could give this past season a mixed review, I'd say, but I think all in all with what has gone on we have to look at it as a success. I know that sounds odd because if you look at the standings we finished fourth, but I think the inconsistency with regards to awarding points for games that weren't played was unfair especially because if the remaining games had gone ahead and results had gone in our favour we could have still won the league."

"I don't think it's a stretch to say we'd have been favourites to win the playoffs for a fourth year in a row back in our own rink either, so I think there are definitely positives you can pull from the season."

"As a whole I think it was a colossal effort from everybody involved; the players, the management and the coaches all pulled together at the back end of the season and it all seemed to be coming together at the right time."

"I think we're all disappointed we weren't able to see the season out and lift another cup for the fans that come week in and week out to watch us play, but at the end of the day, it was the right decision for games to stop when they did, people's health and wellbeing are far more important than finishing the season."

"I have no problem doing the 'less pretty' aspects of the game like blocking shots or putting my body in places I know it's going to take a bit of a beating if I know it'll help the team and I just tried to do that as much as possible and as well as I could."

"I'd have to say, though, as a season it's probably been my most enjoyable so far. We lost a lot of good players from last year coming into this one, that was always going to be hard to replace but we had a great bunch of lads and a lot of character in the dressing room this season, the camaraderie and togetherness of the team made it really enjoyable to be a part of - and I think that's a big reason why we were still in the running for trophies right till the very end."

By the end of the current 2019/20 Laidler Division season, after 5 seasons with the Wild, Dan Bracegirdle had played 122 games, scoring 5 goals and 12 assists, with 150 penalty minutes.

Commenting on his award for having passed 100 games, Bracegirdle said:

"It feels good to have played so many games for the club, it's taken long enough to get there that's for sure! I've been unlucky with injuries and illness over my time at Widnes which has meant that I've often had to miss big parts of the season and twice miss the season entirely, so to finally pass the 100 game marker felt really good."

GW Images / Geoff White
Widnes Wild Official Club Photographer
Tel: 07732 388416 www.gw-images.com

Widnes / Deeside Rivalry - Part 1

First Published in the Widnes Weekly News on 20th August 2020

Calum Ruddick (#19) and Bobby Caunce (#77) put pressure on the Deeside goal in the game away at Deeside on 22 September 2013. (Photo by Geoff White)

After several false starts, ice rinks have finally started to re-open across the country following the further relaxation of government regulations concerning the use of indoor sports facilities in the wake of the coronavirus pandemic

There are a lot of restrictions in place, such as reduced numbers allowed on the ice at any one time and no body contact allowed in ice hockey training, but this development will still come as a great relief to skaters and hockey players who have not been able to get on the ice for almost 5 months.

Competitive ice hockey matches are still a long way off, however, and no announcements have yet been made as to when the new season might start.

There are also question marks as to which teams will be competing and what format the league competition – once it gets underway - might eventually have.

Sadly, one popular fixture in the ice hockey calendar that looks unlikely to take place this season is the Widnes Wild / Deeside Dragons local derby game as the Dragons currently have no home ice.

Their Deeside Leisure Centre home was converted into an emergency hospital to help cope with Covid 19 cases and there are no current plans to re-lay the ice pad. While public health and wellbeing - obviously - has to be the main priority, this will be a bitter blow to the many skaters and hockey teams that use the North Wales facility.

The Widnes/Deeside on-ice rivalry stretches back 7 years to when the Wild team was first founded an d has been a big talking point around the sport since day one.

Fully trained ice hockey players don't grow on trees so any newly established team will always attract players from other local rivals and with the Widnes catchment area falling slap bang between Deeside (22 miles to the west) and Altrincham (21 miles to the east), it was obvious right from the start that a few players from each of those clubs would de-camp and join the new Wild team. Regular player movements between neighbouring teams are very common in ice hockey, and this is how local rivalries build up.

One of the first such players to join the Wild was Calum Ruddick a Manchester based player who had been with the Dragons for a number of seasons. Another early defector from Deeside was Ben Simister, who had been a Flintshire club junior and played the previous 2 seasons for the Dragons senior team and he was installed as the Wild's first team captain.

Looking back at his decision to join the new Wild team, Ruddick said:

"I had left Deeside in the middle of the previous season and had a few months away from hockey. I wasn't enjoying it and, when Widnes came about - and the chance to play with Ken Armstrong, and a few other boys I had played with when I was younger - I didn't want to miss the chance. You could tell from the start that Widnes was going to be a fun place to play. From day one, Gaz Fearon and Pete Bleackley were great with me and all the boys. I think at the

time nobody really expected much from us as a team or club but I'd argue, in time that has changed a fair bit."

The first ever meeting between the two local rivals and, in fact, the Wild's first ever league game of any sort took place on 8th September 2013 at Deeside Leisure Centre. The rink at Widnes was not ready to stage home games at the start of the season so they had to start off by playing away game until the end of October.

Chris Preston put the Wild ahead in the very first minute of the game but the more experienced and numerically superior Dragons hit back and led 4 2 at the end the first period after a Joe Charlton strike had evened the scores again briefly. Shaun Dippnall scored the only goal of the second period to keep Widnes in the hunt but two quick strikes for the home team early in the third edged them further ahead. Wild captain Simister fired in two for Widnes but three late goals flattered the Dragons somewhat with a final scoreline of 9-5.

After the game, Simister said: *"Overall, it was a disappointing result to go into the third period one goal down, and then lose by 4. We were still short benched on our defensive lines so, once we have a full squad and our roster is complete, I'm pretty confident we will be right there with any team in the league. Away at Deeside was always going to be a difficult first game of the season, but we have them again in 2 weeks, so we'll get to work at practice and come out flying next time."*

The second Dragons v Wild came just two weeks later on 22nd September and saw Bobby Caunce top score with 4+1 in what finished up as a 10-7 defeat for Widnes.

The first visit by the Dragons to Widnes eventually came on 19th January but the Wild were unable to make the most of their home advantage. After a close, 1-1, first period with Shaun Dippnall scoring the Wild goal, the visitors ran away with the game in the second with 5 unanswered goals. A goal-less third period left the score standing at 1-6 to the Dragons

By this time, Ben Simister had moved back across the border and rejoined the Dragons and his main contribution to this game involved picking up an entertaining 2+2+10 roughing penalty - along with Wild's Tom Jackson - in the closing minutes in a generally bad tempered game that's saw 90 PIM handed out overall (34-56).

In a season where Widnes visibly improved as time went by, and the fledgling team began to gel, they finally picked up their first win over the Dragons on 16th March 2014 at Silver Blades Widnes.

The score was 1-1 at the of the first period thanks to a Ben Brown strike for the Wild but Widnes then stormed ahead with goals from Filip Supa and Bobby Caunce to lead 3-1 at the end o the second. They went 5-1 up courtesy of strikes by Shaun Dippnall and Caunce again before Deeside eventually found their mojo but three goals in the last 5 minutes for the visitors were not enough to stop Widnes picking up their first ever win over their local rivals.

In the end, one win out of three wasn't too bad a haul over the Dragons, who went on to finish the season in second place in the league table, with Widnes ending up 5th in their first ever season of competition.

The next - 2014/15 - season saw more player movements up and down the M56 with Dragons players Danny Bullock and Matt Wainwright joining Widnes, while former Flintshire junior Aled Roberts switched back to Deeside after playing a few times for the Wild at the end of the previous season, having come back from a stint in Canada.

On 14th September, Widnes picked up their first ever win in Deeside with a feisty 6-7 victory. This game attracted an incredible 174 penalty minutes (Dragons 136 – Wild 38) and three of the Widnes goals came on the powerplay.

The rest of the season followed a similar pattern with the Wild winning all 4 league games against Deeside and each encounter attracting a sizeable amount of penalties. They won 4-2 at home in November and then 5-8 away again in North Wales in December.

The final meeting of the season took place at home on 28th February and this was exceptionally close. After a 0-0 first period, the score was finely balanced at 1-1 after the second – then defenceman Dan Bracegirdle popped up to score what, for him, was a very rare goal with just 5 minutes left to play to secure a dramatic victory - and historic clean sweep for the Wild - and his resulting celebration is still talked about to this day!

Showing an improvement on their first season's performance, Widnes finished the season in 4th place in the league table, with Deeside ending up 8 points behind them in 5th.

Talking about the special feeling associated with local derby games from a player's point of view, Calum Ruddick said:

"The derby games are the ones the boys look forward and the ones you look for when the fixtures come out. I missed the first game with Deeside, and then the next two games they beat us, so going into the final game we played them that first season, we were chasing the play offs and we beat them which was a good one. It's always nice to get one over your rivals, but being an old team and with some of their fans, it adds a bit more to it. Beating them in our own barn, that one felt good!"

"The atmosphere is always good with Widnes and Deeside - the teams feed off it and it makes the games more fun playing in front of a big crowd, especially at Widnes where the fans are on top of you. Deeside have some good fans - some really good guys - but I'd say the Widnes says are by far the best in the league."

"It's fun to play against guys who you know – I'm not sure if it's easier or harder - but there are some players who I would certainly rather play with than against!"

After two seasons of increasingly intense rivalry between these two near neighbours of north-west ice hockey, 8 competitive matches had been played overall. Deeside had won the first three but then the balance in power had swung slightly with Widnes going on to win the next five encounters.

The Dragons had a slight advantage on goals scored, with the count at 43 to 39 in their favour and they were well ahead in terms of PIM with 372 to 176!

Deeside had finished above Widnes in the 2013/14 season when they finished 2nd to the Wild's 5th, while the Wild had finished above the Dragons in the 2014/14 season when the two teams finished 4th and 5th respectively.

If things had already become rather fraught in the short time that the two teams had been pitched against each other, a particularly volatile set of circumstances was set to emerge in the summer of 2015 that would intensify the Widnes / Deeside rivalry even further.

Widnes / Deeside Rivalry – Part 2

First Published in the Widnes Weekly News on 13th August 2020

The home game of 8 November 2014 and Wild's Dan Bracegirdle (#4) and Deeside's Chris Jones continue a long-standing debate. (Photo by Geoff White).

The summer leading up to the 2015/16 season caused much discussion in both the Wild and Dragons camps. Matt Wainwright went back to Deeside after just one season in Widnes and he was joined by import Filip Supa who had also chosen to switch allegiances in a move that many fans saw as the ultimate betrayal.

The arrival of Scott McKenzie as new Wild player coach - and then a batch of new players at Deeside controversially financed by the backing of the Red Hockey media group - suggested that both sets of fans were to be in for a fascinating season.

Widnes made a good start in their first game against Deeside at the Silver Blades rink on 13th September, leading 2-1 at the first period break with goals from George Crawshaw and Geoff Wigglesworth and then going 3-1 up with a goal from McKenzie in the 23rd minute.

However they were outshot by more than to 2 to 1 in the second period and conceded 5 straight unanswered goals to trail 3-6 heading into the third period. By then, the damage had been done. The Dragons came away with a 4-7 victory and Widnes were left playing "catch up" for the rest of the season.

Deeside topped the league pretty much from starts to finish and, while the Wild looked fairly secure in second place, they were unable to take any points off the Dragons to close the gap.

A closer game at Deeside on 8th November saw Widnes narrowly lose 3-2 – the task being made more difficult than it needed to be as McKenzie was the off ice for the crucial last 6 minutes of the game with a major roughing penalty.

Valentine's Day 2016 saw the Wild's best result of the season against Deeside with a highly entertaining 7-7 home draw. It was the only point that Widnes would take off the Dragons all season but the Welshmen still had the last laugh as the result secured them Laidler Division title that same evening.

The fourth and final league meeting between the two teams – played at Deeside on 26th March - finished in a controversial fashion. With nothing to play for except local pride, the Dragons appeared to adopt an unnecessarily overly aggressive approach to the game.

Once again, Widnes scored first through Scott McKenzie but two goals from Adrian Palak saw Deeside lead 2-1 at the first break.

Early in the second period Wild netminder Greg Ruxton suffered a recurrence of an old knee injury after a strong challenge which put him out of action for the rest of the season and he had to be replaced by Widnes Wildcats rec netminder Ian Thirkettle, who had been called up as emergency cover for the game.

Before Thirkettle even had time to get settled, Matt Wainwright scored for the Dragons to put them 3-1 up and shortly after this, Wild's Lee Kemp had to go to hospital to be treated for a head injury after a dangerous check from behind against the boards.

Keen to avoid any further injuries to his players with the play offs just around the corner, coach McKenzie withdrew the team from the ice early. The score at that point stood at 3-1 to Deeside and the EIHA later decided that the Dragons should be awarded the win.

Widnes finished the season in second place in the Laidler Division table – 8 points behind champions Deeside. Deeside had only lost 1 game all season while the Wild had lost three times to them and twice to Nottingham.

The two local rival teams also met in the 2016 play off final at iceSheffield and, once again, it was a case of "so near yet so far", with the Dragons winning 5-3 to secure the league and play off double.

With Dragons winning promotion to the Moralee Division for the 2016/17 season, there would be no league games between the two teams for the following season, but the keen competitive spirit between the two camps would continue all the same.

With the Dragons winning promotion to the Moralee Division for the following season, there were no league meetings between Widnes and Deeside but still plenty of talking points. In June Scott McKenzie suddenly went to join the Welsh outfit as player coach, taking Chris Gee, Geoff Wigglesworth and a couple of "almost" signings - who had just been prepared to put pen to paper for Widnes - with him.

Widnes went on to have a good season in the Laidler Division, finishing second once again with Ollie Barron's new look team, while the Dragons had a difficult time in the higher Moralee Division, winning just 9 out of 28 games and ending up second bottom. This set of circumstances set up a mouth-watering Promotion/ Relegation play off game between the two local rivals as a season finale, to be played on neutral ice in Blackburn.

With Deeside still in the Moralee Division for the 2017/18 season, and Widnes still in the Laidler Division, there were no league meetings again between the two fierce rivals. However, this season, the Deeside club decided to ice a "Dragons2" development team made up of mainly young and inexperienced players to give them some extra match experience and they entered the North 2 division, along with a similarly composed Blackburn team.

There was plenty of Widnes interest in this new "Dragons 2" team with ex-Wildcat and Wild import Michal Fico leading the attack and former Riverside Raiders rec players Owen Tennant, Charles Perry, Dave Priestley, Gez Evans & Sam Plant also lining up for the Welsh side.

While it was good to be able to enjoy some local rivalry again, these matches were all very one sided, with the Wild winning easily on each occasion. They won 11-6 in the first meeting in November and then notched up a club record 2-22 victory away at the beginning of January.

The second home encounter of the season in February brought a 20-1 victory for Widnes and some unfortunate scenes that saw a sackful of penalties handed out and Fico potentially facing a lengthy ban.

The fourth game with the Dragons2 was cancelled due to bad weather and eventually awarded as a 0-0 draw by the EIHA which, apart from their 4 wins over the equally poor Hawks2 team, represented Deeside's only positive result of the season.

During the summer, the Dragons main team dropped back down from the Moralee Division, having had a terrible time all round and finishing rock bottom of the table - and the two Deeside teams combined to play as a single unit in the Laidler Division for the following season.

The 2018/19 season was by far the most memorable for Wild players and fans as they finally won the Laidler Division league title after having come second for the previous three years. They also won all four league meetings against both the Dragons and Altrincham Aces, meaning that they had a complete clean sweep over all their main North West rivals for the first time ever. To be fair, both the Dragons and Aces had poor seasons by their own standards and finished second and third from bottom respectively.

Things started well for the Wild with a 2-5 win away on Deeside in November followed by an 11-4 victory at home in February. By the time Widnes travelled to North Wales again at the end of March they had already secured the league title and were able to celebrate the fact with a 5-9 win - and then were able to rub salt into the wounds a week later, when they received the league trophy after their final home game of the season when they beat the Dragons once again by a whacking 16-5.

The summer of 2019 saw a lot of movement behind the scenes with Widnes appointing Mike Clancy as new head coach following the retirement of Ollie Barron. Clancy had been a netminder with Flintshire Freeze back in the 1990s and had a good reputation as a juniors coach at conference and international level and he brought with him his younger brother - former long term Dragons netminder Dave Clancy - and equipment manager Charles Humphries.

Following the Clancy brothers up the M56 to Widnes were Dragons players Jonah Armstrong and MJ Clancy and also Ryan Kemp – who, although most recently with Bradford Bulldogs, had also played several seasons at Deeside in the past. On the other side, former Riverside Raider Sam Plant was still turning out for the Dragons and was joined by former rec team-mate Mike Rogers who joined the Welsh team as back-up netminder.

The Wild had a very disappointing season overall and Clancy's experimental new look team - a mix of promising young talent and experienced old heads - suffered from many long-term injuries.

The Dragons picked up their first win in Widnes since September 2015 with an all-round surprising 2-4 win on 8th December but the Wild redressed the balance winning 2-7 away in Deeside in early January.

That game was particularly notable for the Dragons players losing their heads once the game had started to run away from them, picking up an eye watering 108 PIM compared to 16 for Widnes.

On 2nd February the Wild edged ahead in terms of local bragging rights with a very close 5-4 win over the Dragons but they lost the final meeting of the season between the two sides 3-2 on 15th March in what was the Dragons' last home game played to date.

Interestingly enough for the Dragons / Wild dynamic, over the course of the season Mike Rogers had been given his chance in goal for Deeside after an injury to their first choice netminder, women's Team GB international Samantha Bolwell, and had given a very good account of himself. He played a blinder against his former rink-mates, turning away 31 of the 33 shots that he faced over the 60 minutes.

That result might have threatened the Wild's late title challenge had the league programme not been curtailed the next day and Widnes, instead, finished the season in 4th place in the Laidler Division table, 9 points ahead of Deeside in 6th.

In Summary

Over the past 7 seasons, Widnes have played Deeside Dragons 22 times (or, in fact, 26 if you include the 4 games against Dragons 2 development side, although that's not really comparing apples to apples...) and, intriguingly, the Wild have won 11games to Deeside's 10. The only ever draw came in the 7-7 game at Widnes on the day that Deeside won the Laidler Division title.

In that time, Widnes have scored 116 goals and conceded 101. The penalty count in games between the two teams is Wild 529 to Dragons 859, although that doesn't count the 3-1 game that was abandoned in March 2016 nor the first ever Wild game away in North Wales on Sept 2013, which wasn't recorded properly for some reason....

Wild players line up away to Deeside on 22nd September 2013: Left to right: Joe Charlton (#68), Chris Preston (#47), Tom McDonald (#37), Mark Higson (#14), Andrew Clark (#5), Craig Williams (#88) (Photo by Geoff White)

Widnes / Altrincham Rivalry

First Published in the Widnes Weekly News on 10th September 2020

Wild's Lee Kemp (#15) and George Swanston (#11) mix up it with some Aces players in a derby game away (Photo by Geoff White)

Widnes Wild games against the Altrincham Aces are always very feisty affairs and are looked forward to by players and fans alike. The current Aces team was only formed in 2015, so the rivalry doesn't stretch quite as far back as with the Deeside Dragons but there is just as much passion involved and you can usually cut the atmosphere with a knife when a Widnes / Altrincham derby is going on.

The Wild actually played against the Altrincham-based higher division Trafford Metros in their second-ever game back on 25th August 2013. It was a one-off challenge game to help introduce the new team to the Widnes public, following on from the game against Sheffield Spartans two weeks earlier.

Interestingly enough, the Metros team that won 5-8 that day included Ben Brown, Lee Pollitt and Geoff Wigglesworth who would all switch to join the Wild for their debut season. Also in the Metros team were Nicole Jackson and Chris Gee who would go on to play for Widnes in later years.

In terms of former Trafford players, the Wild team that day had Marc Etherington, who had been the Metros captain the previous season, Thomas Ratcliffe who had been a Manchester Phoenix junior but had never played for the senior team and back up netminder Tom McDonald in their ranks

Czech import Lukas Zeman did most of the damage in the game as far as the Wild were concerned, opening the scoring for the Metros after just 36 seconds and going on to score 4 goals overall in the 5-8 victory.

Goals from Ben Simister, Richard Charles, Thomas Ratcliffe, Calum Ruddick and Chris Preston kept the Wild in contention but there was never really much chance of the newcomers beating Trafford on this occasion.

The Metros – and their subsequent incarnation of the "Manchester Minotaurs" - played in the higher Moralee Division so there were no more derby encounters in that direction during the Wild's early years. In fact, the next time that Widnes played an Altrincham team didn't come until the 2015/16 season, when the Aces were reformed following the departure of the Manchester Phoenix organisation from their Oakfield Road rink.

The Aces team that season had Joe Greaves – who had spent the previous season at Widnes, Tom Revesz - who seemed to spend a period yo-yoing between the two clubs, and Daniel Etherington who had played a few times for the Wild in their debut season.

The Wild had Shaun Dippnall who had played for the Metros in the 11/12 season, Sheldon Cassidy, Geoff Wigglesworth, Chris Gee, Thomas Ratcliffe, Ben Brown and Tom McDonald - who had all played at Altrincham in the past.

The season started with a 4-2 challenge match win for Widnes and then the Wild won the first league encounter 8-5 at home in November. They drew 4-4 in their first ever away game at Altrincham but then won 2-5 a fortnight later on their second visit.

A 9-1 hammering back in Widnes in early January handed the Wild an unbeaten record in their first season of meetings with the new Aces team.

The 2016/17 season started with back to back challenge games over the August bank holiday weekend. The away game on the Saturday saw Ollie Barron's new look Wild team win 3-6 and then win 4-1 at home the night after.

The league meetings saw 4 very close and competitive matches with a 3-3 draw at Altrincham and 4-2 home win on consecutive weekends in November.

The Aces picked up their first ever win over Widnes with a 6-3 victory in January before losing 7-5 at the end of March in a top four encounter that saw both teams vying for places in the end of season play offs.

That game took the term "rivalry" to a whole new level as, not only was it attended by a sizeable group of Manchester Storm Elite League fans whose own team were without a game and had come along to cheer on the Aces for the night, but there was also a prominent vocal group of Manchester Phoenix fans who had adopted allegiance to the Wild team after their own club had folded mid-season and were there urging on the Widnes team!

It was an especially close game that saw the Aces lead 0-1 at the end of the first period and then 4-5 at the end of the second. A 3-0 final period eventually secured the win for the Wild and they went on to finish second in the Laidler Division table, seven points ahead of Altrincham who came third.

The two teams the met in the Play Off semi final at iceSheffield and this was also a very tense affair. The Aces outshot Widnes by 32 to 27 over the 60 minutes but were unable to find a way past netminder Matt Croyle and the Wild won their way through to the play off final for the second year in a row with two goals from player coach Ollie Barron in a 2-0 shut out.

Season 2017/18 saw the Aces line up with former Wild players Joe Greaves, Sheldon Cassidy, Sam Dunford, Tom Revesz, Lee Pollitt and former Wild women's team player Sarah Hutchinson while the Wild team still had Wigglesworth, McDonald and Ratcliffe in their ranks. They had also made a bit of a coup by attracting young playing talent Mikey Gilbert down the M56.

*Widnes Wild's Mikey Gilbert (#16) with brother Tom and mother Toni
(Photo by Geoff White)*

In fairness to Gilbert, he also had a job at the Planet Ice rink in Widnes and was put in charge of setting up the new Wild Academy junior teams, so it wasn't purely a move based on choosing to play for a better team.

However, having gone all the way through the junior ranks at Altrincham and also making senior appearances for the Metros and Aces for the past 5 seasons, this was quite an upheaval, especially as it would pitch him head to head against his older brother Tom who also played for the Aces – and his mother who was a team official.

The Wild won the first encounter of the season with the Aces in October with a 2-1 overtime victory. The score had been tied at 1-1 after 60 minutes play and the first ever OT period for the Wild saw none other then Mikey Gilbert pop up with the winning goal over his former club 121 seconds into extra time.

The win saw the Wild move briefly to the top of the Laidler Division table but a 2-0 shut out away in Altrincham on Bonfire Night caused them to lose ground to eventual champions Sutton Sting.

A comprehensive 7-2 win at Widnes in January and then a 4-3 defeat away in Altrincham – also an overtime golden goal – meant that honours were shared between the two teams for the season and Widnes finished runners up in the league, with Aces fifth - just outside the play off positions.

The 2018/19 season saw the Wild land another coup with the signing of Czech forward Jakub Hajek, who had played the previous season with the Aces, scoring 26+19 in 32 league games.

With Shaun Dippnall and Chris Gee back with the Wild after brief sojourns elsewhere and Gilbert, Ratcliffe and McDonald returning for the season, this brought Widnes' complement of ex-Aces up to 6 while Altrincham had 5 former Wild players in Dunford, Greaves, Cassidy - along with Kyle Haslam and netminder Phil Crosby.

This was the year that everything finally went right for Widnes and they won the league title at long last after finishing second for three years in a row. They beat the Aces in all four league meetings – 6-1 at home in November, 3-6 and 2-6 away and then 4-1 again at home on 17th March in the game that secured the league title for Widnes.

Following the retirement of successful player coach Ollie Barron in the summer of 2019, the Wild appointed Mike Clancy as his successor and he brought in a longer view policy of encouraging younger players. In came Charlie Ratcliffe – Thomas' younger brother who had played the previous season with the Aces – and former Storm juniors U18s Jake Lowndes and Sam Anderson. Team GB women's international player CJ (Clara) Ashton also played two games for the Wild during the season and her inclusion brought the former Altrincham contingent to 10 overall.

Widnes hammered an unprepared Aces side twice in pre season challenge games – 1-10 away and the 7-2 at home - and they also won 3-5 in the first league encounter at Altrincham in October.

They came unstuck big time with a surprise 3-4 home defeat at the start of November – the first time that the Aces had ever won a game in Widnes - in a match that would be famously remembered for a "was it or wasn't it" goal that was scored as the buzzer sounded for the end of the second period.

After a lot of discussion, the match officials decided that the puck had, indeed, crossed the line milliseconds before the buzzer had sounded – fact that was confirmed later after frame by frame analysis by the Wild's official video-grapher.

Widnes went on to win the next meeting 3-4 away and then managed to lose 3-6 at home in a back-to-back weekend at the end of January and that meant that Altrincham narrowly secured local bragging rights for the season with 16 goals to 15 and two wins each over the 4 matches.

In total Widnes have played Altrincham Aces 26 times in 5 seasons – 20 league games, one play off semi final and 5 challenge matches. The Wild have by far the better playing record overall, having won 18 games, drawn 2 and lost 6.

They have won all 5 challenge matches with a goal tally of 31 to 9 and the competitive games have a combined score of 95 goals to 60.

Talking about the rivalry between Altrincham Aces and Widnes Wild, Mikey Gilbert said:

"With both of the teams being very close to each other a bit of a rivalry is going to crop up. These types of games I always used to - and still do - look forward to the most because there is a bit more intensity in these games and feistiness, which adds to the game and the speed of them which I tend to love."

"The way I see derby games hasn't really changed no matter which side I have played on - they have always had that higher intensity."

When asked whether it felt strange playing against his former club where he grew up, Gilbert said:

"For me it doesn't feel much different, because on both sides I have played with players I like and have friends on my team and also friends on the other team, whether it was while playing for Aces or while I have been playing here."

"The only difference is, I am playing and want to win for the team I am playing for. Everything gets left out on the ice to gain that win for the club. I have friends on both teams still now, however, I put in 100% effort for my team no matter who I am playing against and that is the same for all ice hockey players."

"Its nice to play against people I know and am friends with - and we can catch up after the game but throughout and its the same with anyone, the focus is on the task at hand to win the game."

Widnes & Blackburn Head To Head

First Published in the Widnes Weekly News on 17th September 2020

The Wild score against the Hawks 1 team in the home NIHL Cup game (Photo by Steve Pollitt)

The YKK sponsored Widnes Wild look set to take on the Blackburn Hawks team in the league for the first time in the new season after it was announced that the East Lancashire team are to drop down a division for a period of rebuilding under new owners.

The Hawks have always previously played in the higher Moralee Division so meetings with the main Hawks team - as opposed to second string Blackburn sides – have been relatively rare occurrences

Despite being a little further away than the Deeside and Altrincham ice rinks, Blackburn Arena at some 45 miles from Widnes is still within very easy commuting distances in ice hockey terms and there have been plenty of player movements in both directions up and down the M66 over the years, bringing with it a good deal of local rivalry.

When the Wild team first started in the summer of 2013, Ken Armstrong and Chris Preston signed from the then Blackburn Eagles Laidler Division team and, of the Widnes roster that iced in that first season, Bobby Caunce, Greg Ruxton, Antony Melbourne, Andrew Clark, Troy Evans, Dan Bracegirdle, Dan Etherington, Bradley Valentine, Kurtis Hall, Joe Charlton, Jordan Owen, Marc Etherington, Chad Briggs and, indeed, head coach Mark Gillingham had all trained or played at Blackburn in the past.

With the main Blackburn Hawks team always having played in a higher division than the Wild, meetings between the two have only ever been limited to pre-season challenge games or NIHL Cup encounters, with most games being rather one-sided in favour of the Moralee team.

However, despite having had a mediocre season in the league last year, the Wild actually achieved their best ever results against their lofty neighbours, picking up a win in the preseason games and a competitive point in the cup for the first time ever.

Having played 3 and lost 3 in terms of pre-season games with the Hawks in the past (goals scored 25 to 1…) and lost home and away to the reigning Moralee Division champions and league leaders in the 2015/16 cup (12-2 away and 1-7 at home), it was very difficult to foresee much of a change when it was announced that the Wild would play Blackburn 4 times in the 2019/20 season.

Although the Hawks were no longer the force that they had previously been - and most of their "double double" winning team had either retired from playing or departed for pastures new, the widely acknowledged step up in playing standards between the Moralee and Laidler Divisions suggested that even a "lower half of the table" side should still beat a leading N2 team quite easily.

However, on 7th September 2019, Mike Clancy's new look Widnes squad did the almost unthinkable by beating the Hawks 2-3 on their own ice at the Blackburn Arena in the first pre-season challenge game.

In fairness to the Hawks, it was their first run-out of the season whereas the Wild had already beaten Altrincham Aces home and away the previous weekend but, despite out-shooting the visitors by 51 to 34, the Hawks team – including former Widnes players Joe Greaves, Geoff Wigglesworth, Tom Revesz and Lee Pollitt – were ultimately unable to make the most of their home advantage and their higher standing.

The Wild – with former Blackburn Eagle Ken Armstrong and one-time Hawks player Chris Gee on their bench – kept the score down to a very respectable 1-0 at the first break and then equalised with a goal from new signing Ryan Kemp on 23 minutes. The home crowd were shocked into silence when Widnes took the lead in the 29th minute with a powerplay goal by Michal Novak and the same player went on to edge the Wild further ahead just 32 seconds into the third period.

Blackburn upped their game considerably and peppered Phil Pearson's net with 23 shots in the third period (compared to Wild's 9 on Niks Trapans at the other end), however, the only breakthrough came in the 54th minute when their new import Petr Valusiak finally breached the Widnes defences and that wasn't enough to salvage anything from the game.

The return friendly game the night after at Planet Ice Widnes saw a regrouped and refreshed Blackburn team put in a much-improved performance. Widnes won the "shots on goal" contest by 36 to 31 over the sixty minutes but a 1-4 first period for the Hawks left little doubt as to how the game was going to end up. A 3-3 second period kept the game interesting but 3 more goals for the Hawks in the third – compare to the Wild's single strike – handed Blackburn a convincing 5-10 win overall.

When the two teams met in Blackburn in the NIHL Midland Cup a fortnight later, the Hawks once again held sway with a 6-1 victory, with Shaun Dippnall scoring the only Wild goal of the night.

The return game in the Cup came on 24th November and, with Widnes having lost all of their other cup games at home to Solihull, Sutton and Nottingham - and now struggling with terrible injury problems - not much was particularly expected from this encounter.

However, the brave Wild team battled away and produced what is widely considered to have been their best performance of the whole season, only losing out in the most dramatic fashion in 'sudden-death' overtime having led the game going into the last minute.

Despite only being able to muster 14 players for this game (including two netminders) and the players having to cope with reshuffled and unfamiliar lines, Widnes actually took the lead in the 4th minute with a power play goal from Tom Jackson.

The Hawks equalised 3 minutes later and, following a strike from former Wild player Lee Pollitt, were able to take a 1 – 2 lead into the first break but that was still pretty good from a Widnes point of view, considering the circumstances.

The second period was even closer than the first, with both teams having lots of chances, but it took until 11 minutes in for the next breakthrough. Shaun Dippnall fired in a well-taken equaliser for the Wild and the rink erupted. However, while closely matching their lofty opponents in terms of puck possession and shots on goal, the Wild were unable to build upon this breakthrough and Blackburn re-established their lead on 36 minutes.

Before the game, most Widnes fans would have been over the moon at the thought of "only" trailing the Hawks Moralee Division team by a single goal at the end of the 2nd period but the truth of the matter is the Wild were putting in a superb performance and well and truly deserved to still be in contention at that point.

If the first two periods hadn't been tense enough, the third period was surely a test for the strongest of nerves. Wild's Jakub Hajek pulled Widnes level again, with a goal on 43 minutes but Blackburn struck back again just 60 seconds later, to edge 3 – 4 ahead.

However, Widnes heads did not drop at this setback and they pushed forward again. A second goal of the game for Shaun Dippnall on 47 minutes levelled the scores once again and then an incredible solo break-away goal from Jakub Hajek in the 50th minute put the Wild back into the lead.

A nerve-jangling 10 minutes ensued with Hajek causing the Blackburn defence all kinds of problems and it only looking a matter of time before he scored again.

Both teams had chances but neither was able to find the back of the net. The Wild called a time out with 1 minute 15 seconds left on the clock to discuss defensive contingencies and, with the score still 5 – 4 to Widnes as the game entered its last minute, Blackburn then also called a time out with just 37 seconds left to play.

The atmosphere around the rink was electric and the Hawks pulled their netminder off in favour of an extra attacking player. They piled pressure on the Widnes goal and, unfortunately, the plucky Wild defence were not able to hold out and the Hawks scored a dramatic equalising goal with just 18 seconds left on the clock.

The 5 – 5 draw after the regulation 60 minutes playing time meant that the game went into an extra period of 'sudden death' overtime.

Here again, both teams had chances with Hajek clipping the crossbar for the Wild, before the game was finally settled with a goal from Blackburn's Czech import Petr Valusiak after 1 minute 48 seconds of the overtime period.

While a defeat is always a disappointment, the Wild players were really able to hold their heads up high after such a superb display. It is practically unheard of for a Laidler Division team to beat a Moralee Division team in a competitive game and to have come to within 18 seconds of doing just that was a great achievement for the Widnes team.

While the Wild certainly had a roller-coaster experience in their encounters with the main Blackburn Hawks team last season, their league games in the Laidler Division against the second string "Hawks 2" side were also widely contrasting.

The Blackburn Hawks 2 team were a development side that had been set up to give younger players the chance of getting more ice time and valuable match experience than they would otherwise get if they had to wait on the sidelines in the hope of getting the occasional shift with the main Hawks team. As such, most of their games tended to be rather one-sided affairs and, in the previous two seasons since the Hawks 2 had started, Widnes had beaten them in all 8 of their Laidler Division encounters – with a goals total of 104 to 12.

It came as a bit of a surprise, therefore, that the first meeting between the two teams of the 2019/20 season ran to a completely different script. Due to various fixture reshuffles, the first game with the Hawks 2 didn't take place until 29th December and, even with a severely depleted team, Widnes were expected to win quite easily.

Having had the usual winless season to date, being shut out 9 times and conceding double figures in 11 of their 15 league games, the Hawks had taken advantage of an EIHA rule that allow for under21 players to play for other teams and they arrived with a contingent of Solihull Barons junior players that significantly strengthened their team for the game at Widnes.

Blackburn took a surprising lead on 16 minutes and were still 0-1 ahead at the first break. A straight hat trick from the Wild's Shaun Dippnall eventually put Widnes in the driving seat in the second period but another Blackburn goal on 44 minutes kept things uncomfortably tight.

A Charles Ratcliffe goal on 48 minutes edged Widnes further ahead and blushes were spared when the final buzzer sounded with the Wild still managing to be leading 4-2.

Emma Pearson (#33) in action for the Wild against Blackburn before switching teams in January

(Photo by Hannah Walker)

It was all change for the return game at Blackburn three weeks later as the Wild notched up their highest ever league score with a 0-23 shut out. They outshot the Hawks2 by 134 to 8 and Chris Gee scored 5 goals, with Dippnall contributing 4+5 and Hajek 2+5 and MJ Clancy bagging a hat trick.

In a bizarre twist, Widnes Wild women's team captain Emma Pearson – who had played in the Wild's home game against the Hawks 2 to boost the player strength - actually played for the Blackburn team that night and was named their "Man of the Match".

Pearson signed on for the Hawks 2 for the rest of the season – to help her maintain game sharpness as the Wild women battled for their own league title - and was joined at Blackburn by Riverside Raiders recreational player and Wild women coach Mike Parkin who was immediately named team captain.

The Wild's second league visit to Blackburn on 29th February ended in a predictable - although less dramatic - 1-9 victory in which Mikey Gilbert scored 3+2 and Peter Toth 2+3.

The fourth meeting between the two teams - which had been scheduled for 22nd March - never took place as the league was suspended the week before due to the coronavirus pandemic. The EIHA eventually decided to record all remaining unplayed games as 0-0 draws, meaning that, on paper at least, it turned out be the Hawks 2's best ever result against the Wild.

Wild Break Records In Blackburn
Hitherto Unpublished

Wild's Daniel Haid (#55) is thwarted by Hawks2 netminder Dom Jolly in the 0-23 win away in Blackburn (Photo by Steff Hutchinson / www.steffhutchinson.co.uk)

The Wild's away game against the Hawks 2 team on 19th January was remarkable for several things. Firstly, it saw the Wild notch up their highest ever league win with a 0-23 shut out.

They also fired in a league record 134 shots on goal over the 60 minutes. To put this into perspective – the Hawks 2 game away at Telford when they suffered their highest ever loss of 27-0 on 22nd December only saw them face 97 shots.

The highest ever number of shots in one 60 minute game in the North American NHL is 83 by Boston Bruins against the Chicago Black Hawks in 1941.

Having said that, this means that, by "only" conceding 23 goals from 134 shots, the Hawks netminding duo of Dom Jolly and Bayley Hodkinson actually saved a massive 111 shots on goal which must also be some sort of record itself!

Chris Gee (#46) was the Wild's top scorer in the record breaking game at Blackburn with 5+0 (Photo by Steff Hutchinson/www.steffhutchinson.co.uk)

At the other end, Widnes netminder Tom McDonald was only troubled by 8 shots on goal all game - 4 in the first period, 2 in the second and 2 in the third – all of which he saved to register an impressive shut out.

For those of us who like that sort of thing, reproduced below is the full game sheet for the match, thus preserving these fascinating achievements for posterity.

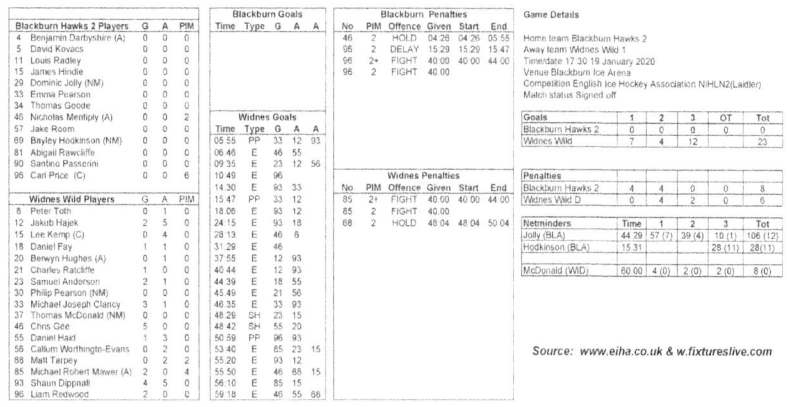

Wild Go To Hull And Back

First Published in the Widnes Weekly News on 15th October 2020

Wild v Hull games are always lively! The last Wild home game before the pandemic lockdown saw Widnes beat Hull 5-4 (Photo by Geoff White)

The YKK-sponsored Widnes Wild have a sense of "unfinished business" with the Hull Jets after last season's truncated league finish and, with the latest news that the Blackburn Hawks team might not, after all, take part in the Laidler Division next season and remain in the higher Moralee Division instead, it means that - assuming both teams are able to ice similar squads to last year - Widnes and Hull are likely to be the top two teams in the North 2 division once again.

Despite being quite a distance away from each other - at some 120 miles and a good two-hour drive or more - a healthy rivalry has developed over the years between the two teams situated at opposing ends of the M62.

Although Widnes have had the upper hand overall in encounters over the past 7 seasons of competition, having won 21 of the 28 league matches – with five wins for Hull and two draws (back in the days when they still had them…) - and have won both of the meetings in the play offs, these games are very keenly anticipated in both camps.

Last season's games between the two teams were especially tantalising, as Hull had their best ever season in terms of league position and ended up winning the Laidler Division title for the first time - a title that Widnes had won the season before and been keen to defend.

But there was a twist in that particular tale that never quiet matcrialised as, in what looked as if it was going to be a fascinatingly tight end to the league season, Hull actually lost their last 3 leagues games – twice against Widnes and once against Bradford Bulldogs - who eventually went on to finish as runners up in the league.

There were 5 points between Widnes and Hull and the Wild had three games left to play – against bottom pair Telford and Blackburn and then at home to Hull on 28th March – and if Hull had lost their other remaining game at home to the Altrincham Aces on 22nd March – as they had 3-6 back in December - that could have set up the mother of all title showdown games at Widnes the week after.

The 12-0 shut out away to Hull on 1st February had been a huge set-back in terms of the title race and was the Wild's heaviest league defeat since a 14-0 defeat away at Solihull Barons in their first ever season back in November 2013.

But Widnes won the second away game in Hull 3-4 on penalty shots after the game had finished 3-3 in normal time and then beat Hull at home 5-4 in the last NIHL game to be played at Planet Ice before the league was closed down due to the coronavirus pandemic. They were finishing on a roll but, sadly, we will never know now what might have happened had that final game taken place.

Back throughout the history of the Widnes v Hull games, there have been dramatic and significant encounters.

In their first season of competition in 2013/14, the Wild had to win their last game of the season in order to finish in 5th place and secure a spot in the end of season play offs. That last game was away at Hull. They won 4-7 with Filip Supa scoring 4 times for Widnes and qualified for the Solihull-based finale tournament.

Having had their heaviest defeat for years away at Hull last season, the year before Widnes had their narrowest ever victory with a 0-1 win away in Hull in December 2018.

The only goal in that tense encounter was scored by Jakub Hajek on 26 minutes in a game where both netminders were outstanding throughout.

That was the season that the Wild won the league and play off double. They only lost 4 league games all season three to the Telford Tigers 2 team and the other was a 4-2 defeat away on Humberside right at the start of the league campaign.

However, most people will remember that season for the excruciatingly nail-biting play off semi final where the two teams were level at the end of normal time, then at the end of 5 minutes overtime and still level after the initial penalty shoot out. The tie then had to go through 4 rounds of sudden death penalties before Shaun Dippnall finally shot home the decisive marker for Widnes to eventually decide a clear winner.

The 2019 play off final saw the Wild and the Jets meet up once again and, while it was a close and entertaining match, Widnes took their 3rd play off crown in a row with a 6-3 victory.

The Wild's record appearance holder Tom Jackson learnt his junior hockey at Hull and played league hockey for the Jets for two seasons before switching to Widnes in 2013. Talking about the rivalry between the two teams, he said:

"There have always been good games between the Wild and the Jets. They are always competitive and, recently, have been some of the toughest games to play.

With the exception of one away game this season against them, both teams have always competed well."

"When the Jets come with 2 lines and have guys skating out 15 minutes into warm ups, we always know we are going to be playing against a team that's going to battle the whole way through the game and give it everything they can - because of the coaching and players they have. Personally, I love those types of games having a good competitive match up for 60 minutes."

"Surprisingly I don't think there are many left who I played with in the juniors. I played at senior level with Jamie Cobley, Andy Ward and Kieran Beach who are part of the core group that keeps coming back every year stronger. I'm so looking forward to getting back to hockey, and just hope with the whole pandemic going on there's a safe way to do so."

NIHL Player Award Winners
Reported on various dates in the Widnes Weekly News

Women's League Player Of The Month Award (19th Dec 2019)

Widnes Wild women's team captain Emma Pearson has been named Oddballs' WNIHL Division 1 North Player of the Month for November.

Awards are made for the top player in all four divisions in the Women's league this season, along with similar awards for the five divisions in the men's competition. Each divisional winner receives an "Obble" hat courtesy of award sponsors Oddballs who manufacture clothing and underwear for men, women and children while at the same time raising funds and awareness for Testicular Cancer.

Nominations for the women's awards are made by the coaches of each team and a monthly choice is made from those nominees. In the case of the men's awards, a short-list is drawn up by a panel of media experts for each division, from which a choice is then made.

Emma is the first Widnes player to receive a league Player of the Month award since Wild player-coach Ollie Baron won the inaugural men's award for the Laidler Division in October 2017. Emma is also the Wild Women's team Player of the Month for November, following on from Stephanie Drinkwater, who won the accolade in October.

Dippnall Named League Player Of The Month (13th Feb 2020)

The YKK Widnes Wild player Shaun Dippnall has been named Laidler Division Player of the Month for January 2020.
Each month a panel of media experts put together a short list of players who have performed particularly well and an overall winner is chosen from that list. There is an award for each of the five divisions in the NIHL and a separate set of awards for the women's leagues, with prizes being sponsored by clothing company Oddballs.

Dippnall is the Wild's leading points scorer for the season so far, with 23 goals and 26 assists, and he sits third in the overall scoring standings for the Laidler Division. During January, he scored 14 goals and 12 assists and was a solid performer throughout the month that saw the Wild win five of their eight League games.

Dippnall is the third Widnes player to win this prestigious league award. Former Wild player/coach Ollie Barron won the inaugural Player of the Month Award back in October 2017 and Widnes Wild Women's Team Captain Emma Pearson won the Women's League Award in November 2019.

Wild Duo Clinch League Awards (3rd April 2020)

The YKK-sponsored Widnes Wild may have had a disappointing end to their Laidler Division season, having been placed in fourth position in the final league table by an administrative decision, rather than on the merits of games played, but there has been a little bit of good news, as first choice Netminder Philip Pearson was voted Player of the Month for February 2020.

The NIHL awards the Player of the Month for each of their five Divisions for each month of the playing season and these are arrived at by a panel of media experts. This is a superb achievement for the Widnes goaltender and, coming straight after the January award for team-mate Shaun Dippnall, shows what a strong finish to the season the Wild were having.

The icing on the cake came when it was announced that Wild Women's team player Leen de Decker was awarded the February Player of the Month Award for the Women's Division 1 North as well.

Former Belgian international appearances record holder de Decker missed most of last season but has been truly inspirational since she returned to the ice earlier in this campaign. She scored 20 goals and eight assists in just seven games, including 4 + 1 in the important 8 – 1 win over Telford and a hat trick in the 2-4 title clinching game away to Solway.

Here again, the Wild Women have featured heavily in the Player of the Month Awards this season as Team Captain Emma Pearson won the Division 1 North Award for the Month of November 2019. By virtue of her nomination for the League award, de Decker is automatically the Wild Women's own Player of the Month for February. Previous winners this season have been: Stephanie Drinkwater (October), Emma Pearson (November), Pauline Hayward (December) and Kat Garner (January).

Shaun Dippnall being presented with the Laidler Division Player of the Month Award for January 2020 by match announcer Paul Breeze (Photo by Geoff White)

Wild women's Leen de Decker was Div 1 North Player of the Month for February 2020 (Photo by Paul Breeze)

Emma Pearson was Women's Div1 N POTM for November 2019 and Phil Pearson was Laidler Division POTM for February 2020 (Photo by Hannah Walker) Ollie Barron was Laidler POTM for September 2017 (Photo by Geoff White)

Dippnall Shortlisted For Player Of The Season (22nd April 2020)

The YKK sponsored Widnes Wild's Shaun Dippnall has been included on the shortlist for the prestigious Player Of The Season award for this year's NIHL North 2 Laidler Division.

Following on from the popular monthly awards – which Dippnall won in January and Wild team mate Phil Pearson won in February - the NIHL are running a Player Of The Season award for each of the 5 league divisions – National, North 1 & 2 and South 1 &2.

Shortlists for each division have been drawn up with three netminders, three defencemen and three forwards from which an overall winner will be selected.

Alongside Dippnall in the Laidler Division nominations, there is further Widnes interest in netminder Mike Rogers who previously played for the Riverside Raiders recreational team and has had a superb season in goal for local rivals Deeside Dragons.

Dippall's inclusion on the shortlist is highly merited. In a rather hit and miss season for the Wild where the team was plagued with injuries and other mishaps, he was a solid performer on the ice and ended up as the Wild's top scorer in the league with 29 goals and 30 assists from 23 games – along with 6 goals and 3 assists in 5 Midland Cup games - all with a highly creditable zero penalty minutes!

Commenting on his inclusion on the shortlist for Laidler Division Player Of The Season, Dippnall said:

"I am very surprised - but also proud to have been nominated. I genuinely didn't expect it."

Looking back over the season – where he finished as the team's top scorer for the first time in his career, he said:

"I actually shouldn't have finished as high as the stats say. I had a few assists more than I should have against my name as there was a glitch on the system. However, I still had a pretty good year points-wise. It was probably the strangest year of hockey in my entire life with the things that were happening behind the scenes, however I still had fun with the boys and managed to bag a few goals along the way!"

"The players were all disappointed with the outcome of the league table. I feel we would have finished in second place with Hull taking the title, rightly so as they were the best and most consistent team throughout the year."

The full shortlist for the 2019/20 Laidler Division Player Of The Season awards is as follows:

Netminders: Dean Bowater (Hull Jets), Mike Rogers (Deeside Dragons), Ian Thirkettle (Bradford Bulldogs)

Defencemen: Ollie Rayne (Altrincham Aces), Boris Giba (Hull Jets), Matt Wainwright (Deeside Dragons)

Forwards: Shaun Dippnall (Widnes Wild), Thomas Humphries (Sheffield Senators), Vlads Vulkanovs (Altrincham Aces).

Wild Players Stage Lockdown Awards Party

With all public events currently cancelled due to the coronavirus pandemic, the most recent casualty has been the Widnes Wild End of Season Presentation evening which had been planned for 18th April.

This is always a highly popular occasion where players, supporters, coaches and match volunteers can all come together in a relaxed social setting to round off the season, present player awards and hand out the "own and loan" shirts that had been sponsored by the fans.

This year's event has been postponed until the government restrictions are relaxed and it is deemed safe for social gatherings to recommence and there are hopes to be able to stage it later in the summer.

In the meantime, Wild player Shaun Dippnall came up with the idea of holding an unofficial awards night - just for a bit of fun - using social media video conferencing, meaning that the players could all link up from the safe distance of their own living rooms, kitchens, conservatories and back gardens.

Some quick polls were hastily thrown together to come up with categories and winners and a fully suited and booted Dippnall MC'd the event. Like all good award ceremonies, it went on for hours and was a really good way for all the players to get together and enjoy some of the camaraderie and banter that they will have been missing out on since the country went into lockdown.

For the record, the winners of these 2020 unofficial "Dippy" Awards were:

Most Valuable Player - Phil Pearson
Best Defender – Daniel Fay
Best Forward – Shaun Dippnall
Players' Player - Mike Mawer
Coaches' Player - Bez Hughes
and Clubman of the Year – Ken Armstrong.

A club announcement will be made once a new date is known for the Wild's Official Presentation Evening and arrangements for voting for the official player awards will be also released nearer the time.

Player Of The Season Award Update

Wild's Shaun Dippnall missed out on the Laidler Division Player of the Season award after the final round of voting.

He had originally been placed on the final shortlist of three for "Forward of the Season" along with Thomas Humphries of Sheffield Senators and Vlads Vulkanovs of Altrincham Aces but the Aces' Latvian import got the final nod in that category.

The "Netminder of the Season" award went to Ian Thirkettle of Bradford Bulldogs – who actually played a couple of games for Widnes back in the 2015/16 season - and "Defenceman of the Season" to Boris Giba of league champions Hull Jets.

The overall "Player of the Season" award for the Laidler Division went to Boris Giba.

Because the women's league season still had over two months to run with many teams having a large number of games still to play when all competitions were stopped, there hasn't been a Women's Player of the Season award scheme this year.

This is a shame as Widnes Wild women's team players Emma Pearson and Leen de Decker would almost certainly have been in contention of the Division 1 North award, having won monthly awards during the season.

S & T SALES & MARKETING LTD

www.sandtsales.co.uk/online-shop

The History of the Swindon
Wildcats 1986 – 2016
ISBN No: 978-0-9530608-7-0
A4 Size - £22.99

The History of the
Bracknell Bees
ISBN No 978-0-9530608-8-7
A4 Size - £24.99

The History of Ice Hockey in
Peterborough
ISBN No: 978-0-9530608-6-3
A4 Size - £19.99

60 Years of the
Altrincham Aces
ISBN No: 978-1-8381165-0-7
B5 Size - 176 pages - £15.99

The Deeside Dragons
ISBN No: 978-1-8381165-3-8
204 pages B5 Size - £15.99

Ice Hockey in Bristol
ISBN No: 978-1-8381165-2-1
B5 Size

The Rise and Fall of the
Manchester Phoenix
ISBN No: 978-1-8381165-6-9
B5 Size

Manchester Storm
The Complete History
ISBN No: 978-1-8381165-4-5
B5 Size

S&T SALES AND MARKETING Ltd

Book Publishing and Engineering Consultants

**For enquiries:
+44 7702035951**

stuartlatham@sandtsales.co.uk
www.sandtsales.co.uk/online-shop

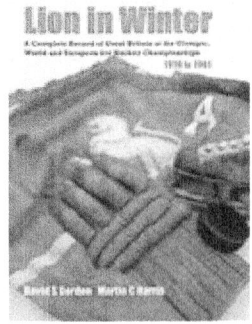

Lion in Winter: A Complete Record of Great Britain at the Olympic, World and European Ice Hockey Championships 1910 - 1981
By David S Gordon & Martin C Harris
Publication Date: 22/09/2019
ISBN: 9781527247475

Lion in Winter is the gripping tale of the Great Britain ice hockey team's fluctuating fortunes, from being the first European Champions in 1910 through to the nadir 0f 1981, when a drop to the bottom of the world rankings resulted in a self-imposed exile from international competition.

A definitive work of record, it is researched and written by two of the game's foremost historians and features the only complete GB Player register ever published, complemented by a wide variety of rare illustrations.

ICE COLD MURDER –
an ice hockey murder mystery
By Michael A Chambers
Publication Date: September 2017
ISBN: 978-0953939831

When a body is found within hockey owner Mark Atkin's establishment, Inspector Dilley has to unravel this terrible scene in order to find out what happened. Amongst a complexity of doors, keys and camera pictures which have much to do with it all.

Many people have much to do with the events that occur this day which puts them 'in the frame' within this much troubled club. Who did it?

Copies available from the author. Contact Michael via e-mail at:
spikc2004@yahoo.co.uk

Brighton Tigers
A Story Of Sporting Passion
By Kevin Wilsher & Stewart Roberts
Published April 2020
ISBN: 978-1-527255-63-0

Brighton Tigers were arguably the most successful and passionately supported ice hockey team in the UK in the years between 1935 and 1965. This book reveals for the first time the remarkable love affair between ice hockey and the sports fans of Brighton, Hove and surrounding towns.

ALSO AVAILABLE FROM THE SAME PUBLISHER

Artists Of
The First World War
ISBN978-1-909643-37-6

Guns & Pencils
ISBN 978-0-953978-22-9

Purple Patches
ISBN: 978-1909643-00-0

Wilfred Owen: Centenary
ISBN: 978-1-909643-36-9

Female Poets - Vol 1
ISBN 9781909643-02-4
126 pages paperback

Female Poets - Vol 2
ISBN 978-1-909643-17-8
186 pages paperback

No Woman's Land
ISBN 978-1-909643-07-9
128 pages paperback

Aviator Poets & Writers
ISBN: 978-1-909643-22-2

The Somme 1916
ISBN 9781909643-24-6
136 pages paperback
with b/w photographs

Arras, Messines,
Passchendaele & More
ISBN: 978-1-909643-21-5 -
150 Pages Paperback

Women Casualties – Vol1
Belgium & France
ISBN 978-1-909643-26-0
86 pages paperback

Poets' Corners In Foreign Fields
ISBN 978-1-909643-08-6
72 pages paperback

Darwen Football Club
ISBN: 978-0953978-24-3

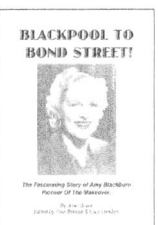
Blackpool to Bond Street
ISBN: 978-0953978-25-0

Colne Giants
ISBN: 978-953978-23-6

Nadja – Complete Poems
ISBN: 978-1-909643-42-0

By mail order from www.poshupnorth.com, Amazon, Kindle, WW1 Publishing and many other quality outlets…!

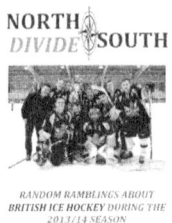

NIHL Yearbook Back Issues Also Available

Available by mail order from www.poshupnorth.com, Amazon, icehockeyreview.co.uk and other quality outlets

Printed in Great Britain
by Amazon